THE HOLY
ROMAN EMPIRE
and Charlemagne
in World History

Jeff Sypeck

Enslow Publishers, Inc.

40 Industrial Road   PO Box 38
Box 398   Aldershot
Berkeley Heights, NJ 07922   Hants GU12 6BP
USA   UK

http://www.enslow.com

Library of Congress Cataloging-in-Publication Data

Sypeck, Jeff.
    The Holy Roman Empire and Charlemagne in world history /
    Jeff Sypeck.
        p. cm.—(In world history)
        Summary: A biography of the Frankish warrior and medieval Christian king who built a great empire in western Europe.
        Includes bibliographical references and index.
        ISBN 0-7660-1901-2
    1. Charlemagne, Emperor, 742-814—Juvenile literature. 2. France—Kings and rulers—Biography—Juvenile literature. 3. Holy Roman Empire—Kings and rulers—Biography—Juvenile literature. 4. France—History—To 987—Juvenile literature. 5. Holy Roman Empire—History—To 1517—Juvenile literature. 6. Civilization, Medieval—Juvenile literature. [1. Charlemagne, Emperor, 742-814. 2. Kings, queens, rulers, etc. 3. Holy Roman Empire—History—To 1517. 4. France—History—To 987.] I. Title. II. Series.
    DC73 .S96 2002
    944'.014'092—dc21
                                                        2001008354

Printed in the United States of America

10 9 8 7 6 5 4 3 2

To Our Readers: We have done our best to make sure all Internet addresses in this book were active and appropriate when we went to press. However, the author and the publisher have no control over and assume no liability for the material available on those Internet sites or on other Web sites they may link to. Any comments or suggestions can be sent by e-mail to comments@enslow.com or to the address on the back cover.

Illustration Credits: Cliché Bibliothèque nationale de France, Paris, pp. 6, 8, 17, 19, 21, 28, 38, 41, 42, 45, 59, 70, 75, 86, 87, 88, 89; Enslow Publishers, Inc., pp. 10, 15, 81, 97, 102; J. G. Heck, *Heck's Pictorial Archive of Military Science, Geography, and History* (New York: Dover Publications, 1994), p. 105.

Cover Illustrations: Enslow Publishers, Inc., (Background); J. G. Heck, *Heck's Pictorial Archive of Military Science, Geography, and History* New York: Dover Publications, 1994, (Charlemagne Portrait).

Contents

Chapter 1

A New Roman Emperor

On November 24, 800, the city of Rome was abuzz. Crowds tried to catch a glimpse as Charlemagne, the king of the Franks, entered the city on horseback. He had come from far to the north, crossing the Alps and riding into Italy. The crowds watched as the great king, dressed in what looked like an ancient Roman toga, dismounted his horse at the steps of the church of St. Peter. Colorful banners fluttered overhead, within view of Rome's ancient ruins. Cheers gave way to the sound of choirs as Charlemagne climbed the marble steps and entered the church.

A few weeks later, on Christmas Day, Charlemagne attended another solemn mass at the church. Pope Leo III, the spiritual leader of the Catholic Church, placed a crown on the king's head. The crowd chanted three times, "To the august Charles, crowned by God,

Charlemagne's coronation made the king of the Franks the new emperor of Rome.

the great and peaceful emperor of the Romans, life and victory!"[1] Charlemagne, a warrior king from a distant land, had become the first emperor of Rome in more than three hundred years.

The Roman Empire

The Roman Empire had collapsed in the fifth century A.D., but its memory was alive and well in 800. The city of Rome had been founded, according to legend, in 753 B.C. Over the centuries, it became the center of a vast empire that had stretched as far as Britain, Spain, and North Africa in the west. In the east, the empire had included Egypt and parts of the Middle East.

After the death of Constantine, Rome's first Christian emperor, in A.D. 337, the empire was divided into two halves: the western empire, with its capital in Rome, and the eastern empire, with its capital in Constantinople (now known as Istanbul, Turkey). The western empire was forced to deal with attacks from various tribes on the outskirts of their borders. These tribes are known as Germanic to historians because they spoke a language related to early versions of modern German. The Romans saw them as barbarians. To the Romans they were also pagans, meaning they worshiped multiple gods instead of a single god like the Christians.

Between 400 and 500, the western Roman Empire was conquered and divided into pieces by these Germanic tribes. Britain was invaded by Germanic tribes from northern Europe. The Roman province of Gaul (today known as France) was conquered and divided by Germanic tribes such as the Franks and the Burgundians. The Romans lost Spain to tribes known as the Suebi and the Vandals. The Vandals also invaded and conquered North Africa.

In the early fifth century, a Germanic people known as the Visigoths invaded Italy and sacked the city of Rome. In 476, the Roman emperor was put to death. To historians, the fall of Rome marks the beginning of the Middle Ages, or the medieval period, in Europe. More than nine hundred years later, the

Early on, the Franks were a small Germanic tribe that often clashed with the Romans.

medieval period would end with the Renaissance ("rebirth"), when Europeans would study and try to revive ancient Roman history, culture, and learning.

But in 476, the people in the shards of the former Roman Empire were faced with a hazy, uncertain future. Only the eastern half of the former Roman Empire—known to historians as the Byzantine Empire—still existed, with Constantinople as its capital. The western empire no longer existed. It was divided into smaller kingdoms ruled by Germanic kings— including Francia, the kingdom of the Franks.

Who Was Charlemagne?

Charlemagne was the king of the Franks. The Franks first appear in history as a tribe living along the lower Rhine River (in what is now southwestern Germany, near Switzerland) in the third century.[2] Under their king, Clovis I, the Franks began to convert from paganism to Christianity at the beginning of the sixth century.[3] For a leader of a people once seen by the Romans as barbarians to be greeted in Rome and crowned emperor was important indeed. This time, the "barbarian" king entered in peace.

Rome, Most Excellent of Cities

By the ninth century, the city of Rome was a shadow of its former self. Four centuries after the fall of the Roman Empire, flooding had made the countryside surrounding the city of Rome very poor for farming. The city walls had once protected nearly one million citizens during the height of the empire.[4] They now held between thirty thousand and fifty thousand people.[5] These Romans lived in clusters along the Tiber River.[6]

Early medieval Rome was a city of Christian churches, around three hundred in all.[7] The city was no longer the major center of trade that it had been centuries earlier. However, a great deal of money still came into Rome as a result of people from all over Europe and Asia who made pilgrimages, or religious journeys, to visit the churches and the tombs of early Christian saints.[8] "O Roma nobilis," a song written

Toward the end of the 5th century, Germanic tribes divided up the land of the fallen Roman Empire. The Greek (Roman) Empire in the east would become known as the Byzantine Empire and would fight to gain some of the former Roman Empire territory back.

during the ninth or tenth century, praises Rome as an eternal city at the center of Christianity:

> *O noble Rome, mistress of the world,*
> *Most excellent of all cities,*
> *Red with the rosy blood of the martyrs,*
> *White with the snowy lilies of the virgins,*
> *We greet thee above all others,*
> *We bless thee: hail throughout all ages.*[9]

The city of Rome was still large by the standards of the ninth century, and it remained the symbolic heart of Europe.[10] For Christians, the city was important because the pope was there. For kings and others who fought for power, the city reminded them how vast and powerful the Roman Empire had once been.

Charlemagne's Empire

As emperor, Charlemagne did not rule from Rome. He visited the city only a few times during his life. Instead, he built a palace in Aachen (a town near the border of Germany and Belgium) and gathered some of Europe's finest scholars around him. As a warrior king, Charlemagne tried to bring much of Europe under his control. As a Christian, he fought fiercely against pagan tribes to expand his empire—and to bring pagans under the rule of Christianity.

Charlemagne was emperor for only the last fourteen years of his life, and his Frankish Empire shattered into pieces soon after his death. But for centuries afterward, his coronation on Christmas Day, 800, was seen as the start of a new religious empire. After Charlemagne's death, his vision of a united, Christian Europe inspired the Holy Roman Empire. The title of emperor moved throughout Europe over the centuries, but the Holy Roman Empire lasted for nearly one thousand years—in forms that Charlemagne never could have imagined.

Chapter 2

Heir to an Empire

The pope was coming. In January 754, King Pepin III of the Franks was living at a royal villa on the Moselle River in what is now western Germany, when he learned that Pope Stephen II was on his way to see him.[1] One chronicle, written by a monk named Fredegar, records Pepin's reaction:

> Hearing this, the king gave orders that he was to be received with glad rejoicing and every mark of attention; and he told his son Charles [later called Charlemagne] to go and meet him and escort him to his presence at the royal villa of Ponthion.[2]

A Frankish villa, a cross between a village and a plantation, was a cold place in winter. The king's apartments were usually built of stone, but most of the other structures were made of wood.[3] Making sure that important visitors were comfortable and well fed required a great deal of work, especially during the winter. The residents always had to be ready for a visit from the king, but the news that the pope was coming surely sent the residents at Ponthion into a frenzy, as they raced to make sure that all of the needs and comforts of the important visitor could be met.

Constantly traveling from place to place was a way of life for the Frankish royal family. Frankish kings were always on the move, not only waging wars, but also visiting villas and monasteries throughout the empire. No better way existed for them to make sure that their orders were being carried out, and it let them use the resources at each of the villas—especially food and other supplies.

Young princes such as Pepin's sons, Carloman and Charles, saw quite a bit of the empire by a very early age and probably learned to appreciate its great size. The Frankish Empire—Francia—covered most of the area that is now France and western Germany. In the eighth century, it was a seemingly endless forest broken only by great rivers like the Seine, the Rhine, and the Meuse, and bordered on the south by the vast, imposing Alps mountain range. Francia was divided into two large regions: Neustria in the west, and Austrasia in the east. Carloman and Charles did not see their father's empire framed by a distant stone window; they saw it from horseback, watching and learning as Pepin played various roles: warrior, judge, politician.

Escorting the pope to a royal villa would have been a very important honor for young Charles, who makes his first appearance in written history with his meeting of Pope Stephen II that winter.[4] Very little is known about his childhood, but Charles, who was about twelve years old at the time of his meeting with the pope, probably had the basic education of a Frankish nobleman: He may have known how to read a little and could probably sign his name. More likely, his education had been more athletic: learning to ride a horse, use a bow and arrow, and hunt with a falcon.[5]

Probably known as Karl to his Frankish-speaking friends and family, this young boy sent to greet the pope would later rule much of Europe for decades.[6] His famous name would pass from history into legend. Historians know him as Charles the Great—*Carolus Magnus* in Latin—but medieval poets and storytellers knew him by the more famous version of his name and title: Charlemagne.

The Long-Haired Kings

Historians call Charlemagne's family the Carolingians. Before the Carolingians came to power, Francia had been ruled by another family for more than two hundred years: the Merovingians. The Merovingians were named for their legendary ancestor Merovec, who died in 456. According to one Frankish legend—a story that was not always repeated by more serious-minded historians in Francia—Merovec's father was a sea-monster that looked like a minotaur, half man and half bull.[7] With their long hair and great beards, the Merovingians were the perfect picture of royal wisdom to the messengers who visited from other lands.

However, by around the year 700 the authority of the Merovingians was beginning to fade, at least in the eyes of some nobles. Each half of the kingdom had its own king, but by 700 much of the power was actually in the hands of important people known in Latin as *maior palatii*—the "mayors of the palace."

Who these very powerful mayors of the palace were and what their exact role was is not known. However, by around 700, they were far more important than the kings themselves, who were only puppets

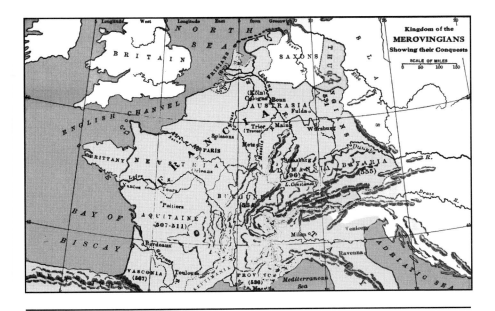

Though they had lost much of their power by 700, the Merovingians had gained a significant amount of territory for the Franks.

of the mayors. Einhard, Charlemagne's friend and author of his biography, provides a vivid picture of how Merovingian glory had faded:

> All that was left to the King was that, content with his royal title, he should sit on the throne, with his hair long and his beard flowing, and act the part of a ruler, giving audience to the ambassadors who arrived from foreign parts and then, when their time of departure came, charging them with answers which seemed to be of his own devising but in which he had in reality been coached or even directed.[8]

Some historians think that Einhard's portrait of the Merovingians was somewhat exaggerated.[9] However, his description does point out the weakness of the Merovingian kings. As their power fell over time, the influence and importance of Charlemagne's ancestors rose.

The Rise of Carolingian Power

Charlemagne's ancestors took nearly a century to capture the Frankish throne. Very little is known about these men from the chronicles that record their names and deeds, but they were clearly very ambitious—even ruthless. They used their roles as mayors of the palace to become the most powerful family in Francia.

Pepin I, who died around 639 or 640, was the powerful mayor of the palace of Austrasia. His family was very active in the murky politics of Francia for decades. His grandson, Pepin II, seized an opportunity around 688 during a war between the two halves of the Frankish kingdom. Because he was an important

Einhard was not only Charlemagne's biographer, but also his friend.

landowner, Pepin II was able to raise an army from among the men who lived and worked on his lands.[10] During the long and complicated conflict, Pepin II took his forces into Neustria, where the Merovingian king, Theuderic III, fell into his hands. Although Pepin II was now the most powerful man in both halves of the Frankish empire, he could not officially rule. The people still wanted a king with Merovingian blood, so Pepin ran the kingdom from behind the scenes while Theuderic III sat on the throne.

Each March, Pepin II would make sure that the Merovingian king appeared at the yearly assembly of all the Franks. But when it was over, the charade ended. The king was sent back to a royal villa "to be guarded," said one later chronicle, "with honor and veneration [respect]"—while Pepin II actually ruled the kingdom.[11]

"The Hammer"

Confusion and war followed the death of Pepin II in 714. The kingdom split in half once again. Amid the chaos rose one of the illegitimate (born before marriage) sons of Pepin II, a man named Charles—later known as Charles Martel, "the Hammer."

Charles Martel was one of Charlemagne's most prominent ancestors. He was the first in his family to be named Charles (or, in Frankish, Karl), giving the Carolingian dynasty its name.[12] Charles was thrown in prison in 715 because his stepmother, Plectrude, wanted to rule by putting her six-year-old grandson, Theudoald, on the throne. But Charles Martel escaped, gathered a small army, and fought to become mayor of Austrasia. After losing many battles, he was at last victorious in 717.

However, the Merovingians were still considered the proper rulers by many of the Franks, so Charles Martel could not make himself the true king of Austrasia. Instead, he ran the kingdom as mayor while a Merovingian king named Chlotar IV sat on the throne. Wishing to control both halves of the Frankish kingdom,

Charles Martel (center), an ancestor of Charlemagne, was known as "the Hammer" for his decisive victories over the Muslims.

Charles Martel invaded Neustria around 719 or 720 and took control of the puppet king there. For several years, he fought against rebels throughout Francia.

But Charles Martel had even larger problems. The religion of Islam had been established in the Arabian peninsula (now known as Saudi Arabia) by the prophet Muhammad, who died in 632. Its followers, known as Muslims, believe that God revealed to Muhammad a holy book called the Qur'an (Koran). Muslims are required to follow religious practices such as daily prayer and fasting at certain times of the year. Islam spread quickly throughout the Middle East and North Africa. By 711, Muslims known as Moors from northern Africa also controlled most of the area now known as Spain. They then began to move into Frankish lands, especially Burgundy and Aquitaine in southwestern France. Because Muslims believe that their religion replaces and corrects the errors of older religions, such as Christianity, the Franks saw them as a threat to their Christian kingdom.

Nobles in Aquitaine had been rebelling against Charles Martel's rule. However, the arrival of the Muslims alarmed their leader, Duke Odo, so he requested Charles Martel's help. In October 732, after seven days of fighting, their combined armies defeated the Muslim forces in a famous battle just north of Poitiers.

To the Carolingians, the victory was important for religious reasons. European Christians saw the Muslims as enemies of their religion, so the Franks saw the victory in 732 as proof that God was on their side. In the Old Testament of the Bible, Judas Maccabaeus, known as "the Hammerer," defeated the Syrians with God's help. As a result, the monks who wrote Carolingian history after Charles Martel's death gave him the name Martellus, Latin for "the Hammer."

Charles Martel Divides the Kingdom

When the Merovingian king, Theuderic IV, died in 737, Charles Martel did not try to replace him with a new Merovingian. Instead, he simply ruled in the dead king's name.[13] In 739, two years before his death, he

The forces of Charles Martel combined with those of Duke Odo to defeat invading Muslims at the Battle of Poitiers in the Frankish region of Aquitaine.

made his two sons, Pepin III and Carloman, joint rulers of the Frankish Empire.

When Charles Martel died in 741, people were suspicious of his sons. Although he had ruled the kingdom with his actions, Charles Martel had not officially been king. Because many Franks still believed that only a Merovingian could be the real king, Pepin III and Carloman found a Merovingian and crowned him King Childeric III. Once again, the king was another powerless puppet who was only trotted out for special events.

In 747, Carloman did a surprising thing. He had been fighting a series of wars against the enemies at the borders of the Frankish Empire, such as the Saxons, a Germanic people in what is now northeast Germany. However, according to one chronicle, Carloman was "burning for the contemplative life."[14] Tired of the hectic, violent life of a Frankish leader, the warrior Carloman exchanged his sword and armor for the rough robes and the simple life of a medieval monk. He soon traveled to Rome and became a monk in central Italy. Nine years later, he grew ill and died peacefully in 755.

Meanwhile, in the violent world Carloman had left behind, his brother Pepin III was sole ruler of the Franks—and only a weak Merovingian king stood in the way of total power.

Mayors Become Kings

At long last, the tradition of pretending that the Merovingian kings were the true rulers was coming to an end. In 749, Pepin III sent a bishop and a priest to Pope Zacharias in Rome with a question about kingship. It was common to ask for advice from the pope, but Pepin III was looking for a specific answer. According to the *Carolingian Chronicles*, he got his wish:

> Pope Zacharias instructed Pepin that it was better to call him king who had the royal power than the one who did not. To avoid turning the country upside down, he commanded by virtue of his apostolic authority [his position as pope] that Pepin should be made king.[15]

In 750, Childeric III, the Merovingian king, was given a tonsure—the special round haircut of a monk—and sent off to a monastery. This act ended the rule of a family that had impressed the people with its long beards and flowing hair. A Carolingian was finally the true king of the Franks.

A Papal Visit

In 754, when Pepin III sent his son, the future Charlemagne, to escort the new pope, Stephen II, to their villa, both the king and the pope had their own reasons for meeting. Some Franks resisted the rule of Pepin III, often with violence. The new king needed the approval of the pope. The pope was not only the spiritual leader of the entire Catholic Church, but he was also seen as God's representative on earth. According to one chronicle, the pope anointed Pepin and also anointed his two sons, just as King David was anointed in the Old Testament of the Bible. This act was meant to send a message to the Franks that the rule of the Carolingians came directly from God himself.[16]

The meeting also helped the pope, who had his own problems back in Rome. The Lombards, who ruled a large kingdom in northern Italy, wanted to control the entire Italian peninsula. So in 755 and 756, King Pepin came to the pope's aid by invading Italy—beginning the long involvement of his family with the Lombards.

An Empire Divided

In 768, after a series of wars against his enemies at the empire's borders, Pepin III became ill with a fever.

Just as his father Charles Martel had divided the kingdom among his two sons, Pepin III did the same. It was a complex arrangement. Charlemagne received Austrasia. Neustra was divided; Carloman ruled most of it, except for a small strip given to Charlemagne. Carloman received the provinces of Burgundy, Provence, Septimania, Alsace, and Alamannia. They both ruled the often-rebellious Aquitaine.

Charlemagne, about twenty years old, spent his first Christmas as king of the Franks in the royal villa at Aachen. The holiday passed quietly. But trouble was brewing in Italy, the clouds of war hung over Aquitaine, and the two royal brothers would soon be at odds. Family disputes would change the Frankish kingdom as Charlemagne dealt with enemies both inside and outside its borders.

Franks and Lombards

When rebellion arose in Aquitaine in 769, Charlemagne responded quickly. The king wanted to thwart the rebellion with the help of his brother Carloman, but when the two met at the town of Duasdives (now Moncontour de Poitou in south-central France), Carloman left abruptly.[1]

Carolingian historians were loyal to Charlemagne and his family, so they tended to write down very little that would cast the king in a negative light. Einhard, ever loyal to his friend and king Charlemagne, suggests that Carloman was unhelpful and did not provide the support that he had promised.[2] What the two men talked about at Duasdives is not known—but Carloman's reign over half of the Frankish Empire would not last long.

Marriage Alliances

Without Carloman's help, Charlemagne led an army into Aquitaine and conquered the forces of Hunold, the rebel leader. But even as trouble lurked in the dark forests of eighth-century Francia, Charlemagne and Carloman also received a call for help from their friends in Italy.

Several years earlier, Charlemagne's father had helped Pope Stephen II against the Lombards, who ruled much of northern Italy. The Lombards had said that they would return certain lands to the pope because they did not want the Franks to invade. However, in 768, Pope Stephen II died and was followed by a new pope, Stephen III. The Lombard king Desiderius did not honor the promises he had made to Pope Stephen II. He also insulted the new pope by trying to make one of his own friends bishop of the city of Ravenna. Pope Stephen III, as the head of the Church, was against the idea and wanted to decide who would serve as bishop.

At this point, a surprising diplomat stepped in: Queen Bertrada, mother of Charlemagne and Carloman. Bertrada met with Carloman—and then took a long journey to Italy.[3] The monks who wrote the *Carolingian Chronicles* are silent about what Bertrada and Carloman talked about, but her plan soon became clear. Charlemagne was already married to a woman named Himiltrude and had a son with her. However, his mother had arranged for him to marry the daughter of the Lombard king.[4] Charlemagne's marriage to the Lombard princess would be worthwhile for both sides. King Desiderius would join his family with the royal line of the Franks; in return, he agreed to stop defying the pope.

For Carloman, who was struggling to keep his hold over half of the Frankish kingdom, the new arrangement was especially chilling. A duke named Tassilo ruled Bavaria, which was on the eastern border of the Frankish Empire. Tassilo was married to another Lombard princess, which meant that he was now related by marriage to Charlemagne.[5] Charlemagne, the Lombards, and the Bavarians were all united by bonds of marriage. They formed a new and powerful alliance—one that encircled much of Carloman's territory.[6] Charlemagne was clearly getting ready to rule the entire Frankish kingdom.

The Death of Carloman

On December 4, 771, the situation in Francia suddenly changed: At the villa of Samoussy (near the modern border of France and Belgium), Carloman died at the age of twenty. Einhard says only that Carloman "died of some disease."[7]

Was Carloman murdered by Charlemagne's allies? Most historians think probably not. The marriage alliance between the Lombards, the Bavarians, and the Franks was deliberately directed toward reducing Carloman's power. Most historians believe that his death was a sudden shock that made all of the planning useless. Others, however, believe that Carloman was ill for a long time and that his death was not sudden. They point out that he did not travel as often as Frankish kings usually did, and he also issued very few letters and laws during this time.[8] Knowing that Carloman was dying, Charlemagne simply could have been preparing to take over the entire kingdom.

Upon the death of his brother Carloman, Charlemagne (pictured) became the sole ruler of the Frankish kingdom. (Although some of the symbols in the background look like Nazi swastikas, the swastika was simply a variation of the cross in the Middle Ages and not the symbol of evil it is today.)

The Lombards Defeated

The alliances that Bertrada built fell apart very quickly. Charlemagne had sent some Franks to the pope's palace in Rome to protect and advise him. However, the Lombards wanted to control all of Italy. Pretending to be religious pilgrims, some Lombard leaders traveled to Rome. They hoped to influence the pope to make decisions that would benefit them, so they replaced the Franks at the palace and became the pope's new, uninvited advisors.[9]

Pope Stephen III died in January 772. He was replaced by Pope Hadrian I, who wrote to Charlemagne for help against the Lombards in 773. Showing his disloyalty to his son-in-law Charlemagne, the Lombard king Desiderius asked the new pope to say that Carloman's infant son should be king of Carloman's lands instead of Charlemagne.[10]

In response, Charlemagne sent his Lombard wife back to her father Desiderius. According to Einhard, this was one of the few times the king ever fought with his mother, who had put together the marriage alliance. One possible reason for the divorce is given by a monk named Notker who wrote a biography of Charlemagne about 100 years later. He claims that the young woman could not have children.[11] However, it is more likely that since Charlemagne had married the Lombard princess only for political reasons, she was simply no longer useful now that the alliance was falling apart.

Near the end of 773, Charlemagne held a council of Frankish leaders and divided his army in half. His uncle Bernard—Charles Martel's brother—commanded one division, and Charlemagne himself led the other. The Lombards might have been able to stop one of the armies, but they could not stop both.[12] At the end of 773, the armies crossed the Alps using two separate passes and met in a valley on the other side. Desiderius fled to the city of Pavia. The Frankish Army followed him and surrounded the city.[13]

The act of surrounding a city and keeping people from getting in and out until they surrender is known as a siege. The siege of Pavia was very risky for the Franks. They could not retreat if things went poorly. The Frankish Army had slowly marched into Italy with heavy, horse-drawn carts full of supplies and tools covered with leather to keep everything dry during river crossings.[14] In the winter, the main passes through the Alps and back into Frankish lands would have disappeared under piles of mountain snow. Laying siege to a city was a long, slow process that involved destroying crops and surrounding the city with war machines such as battering rams and catapults.[15] Sometimes a city could be taken by force, but often the key was to keep enemies trapped inside a city and weaken them with hunger.

In 774, after nearly ten months, Pavia finally fell.[16] Charlemagne's father had been unable to take the city in a siege nearly ten years earlier, but this time Desiderius and his men, who were probably cold and

Source Document

Then could be seen the iron Charles, helmeted with an iron helmet, his hands clad in iron gauntlets, his iron breast and broad shoulders protected with an iron breastplate: an iron spear was raised on high in his left hand; his right always rested on his unconquered iron falchion [sword]. The thighs, which with most men are uncovered that they may the more easily ride on horseback, were in his case clad with plates of iron: I need make no special mention of his greaves [armor to cover the shins], for the greaves of all the army were of iron. His shield was all of iron: his charger was iron coloured and iron-hearted. All who went before him, all who marched by his side, all who followed after him and the whole equipment of the army imitated him as closely as possible. The fields and open places were filled with iron; the rays of the sun were thrown back by the gleam of iron; a people harder than iron paid universal honour to the hardness of iron. . . .

Now when the truthful Otker saw in one swift glance all this which I, with stammering tongue and the voice of a child, have been clumsily explaining with rambling words, he said to Desiderius: "There is the Charles that you so much desired to see": and when he had said this he fell to the ground half dead.[17]

Around 884, a monk from St. Gall, most likely Notker the Stammerer, wrote a description of the king's arrival at the gates of Pavia. It includes this fictional conversation between Desiderius and a Frankish traitor named Otker.

starving, surrendered to the Frankish Army. Soon, the Lombards who ruled cities throughout Italy also surrendered to Charlemagne.

Desiderius probably expected that he would only have to swear allegiance to Charlemagne and pay tribute.[18] However, Charlemagne's patience for the Lombards had clearly worn thin. Desiderius and his family were exiled into Francia, and Charlemagne gave himself a new title: *Rex Langobardum*—"King of the Lombards." Afterward, Lombard dukes sometimes rebelled against the Franks, but they were never again a major threat. Northern Italy now belonged to Charlemagne.

The king had conquered a nagging enemy, but the years that followed were far from peaceful. At the eastern borders of the Frankish Empire, the Saxons were a threat that Charlemagne could not ignore. His wars against these long-standing enemies would lead to some of the most brutal fighting of his entire reign.

Chapter 4

At War With the Saxons

"No war ever undertaken by the Frankish people was more prolonged, more full of atrocities, or more demanding of effort" than the Saxon wars, wrote Einhard. He described the Saxons as ". . . ferocious by nature. They are much given to devil worship and they are hostile to our religion. They think it no dishonour to violate and transgress the laws of God and man."[1]

The Saxons had been known to the rest of Europe for centuries. During the second century A.D., the Greek geographer Ptolemy wrote that they lived near the North Sea. At the end of the third century A.D., the Saxons made themselves known to the Romans when they attacked southeastern England and the northern coast of what is now France.

Named for the short knife—*seah*—carried by each warrior, the Saxons were a Germanic people distantly related to both the Lombards and the Franks. In 612, they had served in the army of Theudebert, ruler of the Austrasian Franks.[2] For nearly two centuries they had paid tribute to the Frankish kings by giving them five hundred cows per year and serving in the army. However, they were not reliable allies to the Franks. In response to Saxon raids, Charles Martel invaded their lands at various times between 718 and 738. For a while during the reign of Charlemagne's father, Pepin III, the Saxons refused to pay the five hundred-cow tribute.[3]

Saxons at the Borderlands

By the time Charlemagne was sole ruler of the Franks, the Saxons were a major threat to his kingdom. Their population had been growing and pushing on the northeastern borders of Francia. But for the Franks, proud Christians with strong ties to the pope in Rome, the Saxons were troublesome also because they were pagans. Einhard describes Charlemagne as a devout Christian from an early age and says that as a grown man the king attended church morning and night.[4] As a Christian, Charlemagne did not trust any promises the Saxons made, since they swore on their weapons rather than swearing to God. The Franks felt that they could break the Saxons only by first converting them to Christianity.[5]

During Charlemagne's first campaign into Saxony in 772, the king destroyed a mysterious Saxon shrine called the Irminsul—possibly a large tree.[6] By destroying the shrine, the Franks were hoping to weaken the

Saxons by making them lose faith in their gods. The Franks found a wealth of gold and silver at the Irminsul, but according to one chronicle, the *Royal Frankish Annals,* at first they could not destroy it completely because they lacked water. The chronicle then says that a miracle occurred: A stream suddenly appeared, to quench the thirst of the entire army.[7]

Early medieval histories contain many of these sorts of miracle stories. Whether or not the miracle actually occurred is unknown, but clearly Charlemagne had destroyed a place that was extremely important to the Saxons' pagan religion. The following year the Saxons fought back. They attacked Frankish lands and tried to burn a church that had been built by a famous missionary, St. Boniface. The missionary had been murdered by pagans in 754.

When Charlemagne learned about the attack on Boniface's church, his patience was gone. He began a major invasion of Saxony.[8] He captured an important Saxon fortress and took control of both sides of the Weser River, an important Saxon boundary. Charlemagne took part of the army farther east to the Oker River. Many Saxon tribes came forward to surrender to the Franks. They offered some of their own people as hostages to show that they could be trusted.

Rebellion on All Sides

At the end of 775, some Saxons snuck into the Franks' camp and caught them asleep, killing many of Charlemagne's soldiers. In response, Charlemagne

Source Document

The Saxons began to attack this church with great determination, trying one way or another to burn it. While this was going on, there appeared to some Christians in the castle and also to some heathens in the army two young men on white horses who protected the church from fire. Because of them the pagans could not set the church on fire or damage it, either inside or outside. . . .

Afterward one of these Saxons was found dead beside the church. He was squatting on the ground and holding tinder and wood in his hands as if he had meant to blow on his fuel and set the church on fire.[9]

This miracle story takes place during the Saxons' attack on the Franks in 773. It deals with Saxons who tried to destroy the Christian church built by St. Boniface. Modern readers usually find these stories far-fetched, but medieval monks took them very seriously and saw them as signs that God was on their side.

continued his long series of battles against the Saxons, defeating them through bloody slaughter, taking hostages, and marching away with treasure. The Franks and the Saxons fought bitterly, taking and retaking the same pieces of ground from each other. When Charlemagne returned to Francia at the end of

775 to pass the winter, both he and his forces were cold and numb not only from the climate of Northern Europe, but also from months of fighting.

In 776, Charlemagne marched into Italy to fight against rebels in Lombardy. When he came home to Francia, a messenger arrived with bad news: There had also been a rebellion among the Saxons, causing the Franks to lose an important fortress called Eresburg.[10] The Saxons then marched west, hoping to conquer the Frankish fortress of Syburg. One version of the *Royal Frankish Annals* records another miracle: The Saxons saw two red shields, wrapped in flames, spinning over a church.[11] According to this story, the Saxons fled in fear and the Franks slaughtered them as they retreated. However, based on another version of the *Royal Frankish Annals* that does not include the miracle story, modern historians believe that the Saxons were simply surprised by a last-minute attack by Franks inside the fortress.[12]

Charlemagne then led his forces deep into Saxon territory, breaking through their lines of defense. The Saxons were weary of fighting. On the banks of the River Lippe, crowds of people came with their families to surrender and be baptized.[13] Baptism is a ritual in which Christians publicly proclaim their faith. By making it look like they were giving up their pagan religion, the Saxons showed that they were surrendering. However, they did not necessarily take their new religion to heart.

Beginning in 772, the Franks, under Charlemagne, would battle the Saxons for thirteen years.

An Assembly at Paderborn

Every year, the Franks held an assembly. In 777, Charlemagne decided to hold it in Paderborn, a fortress deep within Saxon territory—a very clear way to tell his enemies that he planned to keep their lands. Some Saxons attended the assembly, but the true surprise guests were Arab messengers. They had come all the way from Spain to ask for Charlemagne's help against their enemies. The offer they made Charlemagne would turn out to be disastrous, and the king would suffer one of the worst defeats of his entire reign.

Chapter 5

Expanding the Empire

In 756, a Muslim named 'Abd al-Rahman I, one of the last survivors of a powerful family in the Middle East called the Umayyads, traveled from North Africa to try to take control of Spain—which was known to the Arabs as al-Andalus. He made the city of Cordoba his base and spent the next twenty years crushing the other Muslims who occupied Spain. In 776, after defeating his enemies on the rest of the peninsula, 'Abd al-Rahman I was ready to move into northeastern Spain.[1]

Arab Messengers Come to Paderborn

The Muslim rulers of the Spanish cities Saragossa and Barcelona did not accept defeat quietly. They sent messengers to Charlemagne's villa at Paderborn to ask for his help against 'Abd al-Rahman I.

Charlemagne's famous grandfather, Charles Martel, had defended the kingdom against Muslims at Poitiers forty-four years earlier. Christians in Europe remained proud of the victory and still saw Muslims as enemies. However, Charlemagne agreed to team up with the rulers of Saragossa and Barcelona. Befriending rebellious Muslims in Spain could have been very useful to Charlemagne—if he had been able to capture new lands and expand the Frankish Empire.

Failure and Defeat in Spain

In 778, Charlemagne's army—which included Franks, Aquitainians, Bavarians, and even Lombards—marched into Spain and captured the Spanish city of Pamplona. However, matters had changed between the various Muslim rulers. At cities such as Barcelona and Saragossa, the Franks were turned away. One of the leaders at Barcelona named Sulayman al-Arabi, who had originally asked for Charlemagne's help, did not respond now that the king was in Spain. Another leader, at Saragossa, had been murdered.[2] Charlemagne's forces could make no progress, and their reason for being in Spain was no longer clear. Frustrated, they began their retreat.

The homeward journey of the Franks began at the Pyrenees, the imposing mountain range that separates Spain from the rest of Europe. Charlemagne's forces tried to slip through the Pyrenees at a pass called Roncesvalles. What happened next stunned the Frankish Army and was remembered for centuries.

Though Charlemagne and his army defeated Spanish Muslims at Pamplona, they soon found that the Muslim rebel leaders that sought their help either no longer needed it or had been killed.

On the night of August 15, 778, a local people known as the Basques attacked the Frankish Army's rear guard. Charlemagne's army, traveling slowly and with a great deal of equipment, was not ready to fight lightly armed attackers who knew every inch of the mountains. The Basques separated the rear guard from the rest of the army, slaughtered many of the

The Battle of Roncesvalles was made famous by the 11th century French poem The Song of Roland.

Franks, and plundered the carts that carried all of the supplies.

More than three hundred years later, the battle at Roncesvalles reappeared in French literature. *The Song of Roland,* written down just before 1100, is an epic poem that retells the battle—but in a way that Charlemagne would not have recognized. Although Charlemagne was only about thirty-eight years old at the time of the battle, in *The Song of Roland* he is a wise and ancient king with a flowing gray beard. The battle is no longer simply a small battle, but a huge war between Muslims and Christians caused by a Frank named Ganelon. When Roland, Charlemagne's nephew in the poem, is killed in the ambush, the king takes bloody revenge with the help of God's angels— even though in reality the attack was never avenged. The anonymous poet has added many layers of legend to the tale, turning one of Charlemagne's worst defeats into a mighty work of heroic fiction.

Trouble in Saxony

While Charlemagne was in Spain, the Saxons took advantage of his absence and attacked the Franks. Urged on by a leader named Widukind, the Saxons attacked Frankish locations on the Rhine, burning churches and monasteries.[3] Charlemagne responded with Frankish troops. The Saxons ran, but the Franks tracked them to the Eder River. Many Saxons were killed in the battle, and the rest returned home in disgrace.[4]

In 779 and 780, Charlemagne again attacked the Saxons. In the end, many of them were forcibly baptized on the banks of the Oker River. Charlemagne spent Christmas in 780 at his royal villa in Pavia—and planned an important journey to Rome for Easter.

A Visit to Rome

Charlemagne's Easter visit to Rome in April 781 was not meant only to show his friendship with Pope Hadrian I. It was also an important part of Charlemagne's plan for the future of the Frankish kingdom.

Charlemagne had several children by a woman named Hildegard. Their sons were named Charles, Carloman, and Louis, and their daughters were Rotrud, Bertha, and Gisela. Charlemagne also had another son, Pepin the Hunchback, whose mother was a woman named Himiltrude. Charlemagne preferred his children by Hildegard. He wanted to make sure that Pepin, even though he was the oldest of the sons, would have no role in the Frankish Empire.[5]

During the Easter visit, the pope became Carloman's godfather and baptized him—not under the name Carloman, but with a new name: Pepin. (Historians call him Pepin of Herstal to tell him apart from the elder Pepin.) With this act, both Charlemagne and the pope were saying that the oldest son, Pepin the Hunchback, was not worthy of being called such a historic name—the name of Charlemagne's ancestors who had brought the Carolingian family into power. The pope, as God's representative on Earth, favored the newly named Pepin. The elder Pepin, the Hunchback, had been replaced.

Dividing the Kingdom

After the baptism, Pope Hadrian also held a ceremony much like the one Charlemagne had been a part of during his childhood visit to Rome. During that ceremony, Charlemagne, his father, and his brother had all been anointed by the pope. At this new ceremony, Pepin of Herstal was declared King of the Lombards. The younger Louis was declared King of Aquitaine. Their older brother Charles was granted the core of the Frankish kingdom, as well as Saxony.

Charlemagne divided his empire. Each of his three sons was anointed by Pope Hadrian I and given part of the Frankish kingdom to rule. However, Charlemagne still retained most of the ruling power.

Although these children now held royal titles, none of them was yet old enough to rule. Charlemagne ruled the Franks just as he had before.

Why did Charlemagne divide up his empire in 781? His father and grandfather had done the exact same thing, so by this time it was a Frankish tradition. However, Charlemagne was wisely attempting to show, while he was still young, how he wanted the Frankish Empire to be ruled in the future, so that there might be less fighting after his death. He made it clear that only the sons of Hildegard had his permission to rule, and that others—such as Pepin the Hunchback—should not be seen as heirs to the Frankish Empire.

The division also may have been meant to calm some of Charlemagne's subjects at the empire's borders. Like all Frankish kings, Charlemagne was always on the move, and people in places like Aquitaine and Lombardy may not have liked being ruled by a king who was always so far away. Even though Charlemagne's sons were young children, the Franks could still hold courts for the kings in those areas. As a result, the local people might feel like their king was aware of their day-to-day concerns.[6]

Defeat at the Süntel Mountains

After Charlemagne returned to Francia in 782, the Saxons rebelled again. Frankish scouts found the Saxons making camp on the north side of the Süntel Mountains, not far from the modern border of present-day Germany and the Netherlands. Their scattered and disorganized attack on the Saxons is described in the *Royal Frankish Annals*. It is one of the most pathetic military defeats in Frankish history:

> They took up their arms and, as if he were chasing runaways and going after booty [treasure] instead of facing an enemy lined up for battle, everybody dashed as fast as his horse would carry him for the place outside of the Saxon camp, where the Saxons were standing in battle array. The battle was as bad as the approach. As soon as the fighting began, they were surrounded by the Saxons and slain almost to a man.[7]

Several important Frankish noblemen were killed in the battle. In response, Charlemagne gathered as much of his army as he could and marched into Saxony.

As they had done many times before, the Saxons surrendered in 782. But Charlemagne, enraged, had no intention of accepting their word and traveling home to Francia. Even by the brutal standards of the Saxon wars, Charlemagne's orders were very cruel: In the heart of Saxony, where the Aller and the Weser rivers meet, Charlemagne's troops beheaded forty-five hundred of the rebellious Saxons.[8]

Defeating the Saxons

For the next two years, Saxon revolts sprang up everywhere, and Charlemagne fought all over Saxony in 783. Although the Franks rarely fought in winter, when traveling was treacherous and food was scarce, Charlemagne and his son Charles decided to stay in

Saxony during the winter of 784 and into 785—a sign of the king's great frustration with the seemingly unbeatable Saxons.

This time, the Franks were relentless. In 785, they attacked the Saxons everywhere, giving them no time to rest, until they had captured many Saxon forts and villages. That year, the Frankish Army marched through Saxony along open roads. The remaining Saxon forces did not resist them.[9]

But for the Frankish king, whose war against the pagan Saxons had been as much about religion as it was about military conquest, one last thing had to happen before he could declare victory. In 785, at the Frankish villa of Attigny (near the modern border of France and Belgium), Widukind and the other Saxon leaders were baptized and became Christians. At last, after thirteen years of bloodshed and mayhem, Charlemagne had defeated the Saxons.

The baptism of Widukind led to a peace between the Franks and the Saxons that lasted for nearly ten years. Elsewhere in Europe, Charlemagne continued to expand his empire through military conquest.

Charlemagne Expands the Empire

In 785, a Frankish army from Aquitaine crossed the Pyrenees at their eastern end and took the city of Gerona, near the Mediterranean coast—giving the Franks a small foothold in Spain.[10]

In 786, another of Charlemagne's armies fought in Brittany, a peninsula in what is now northwestern

France. As their name suggests, the Bretons were originally from Britain and were descended from the Celts, the ancient inhabitants of Europe. When the Saxons and other Germanic tribes invaded Britain around the year 500, the Bretons fled across the English Channel and called their new home Brittany—"Little Britain." The Bretons had been loyal subjects of the Frankish kings in the past, but in 786, they refused to pay their yearly tribute. Led by a close friend of Charlemagne named Audulf, a Frankish army moved into the swamps and forests of Brittany.[11] Small wooden defenses were no match for Frankish soldiers who had battled Saxons for more than a decade. The Bretons were quickly conquered.

That same year, Charlemagne also took more of Italy, capturing the cities of Benevento and Capua south of Rome on the western coast of the peninsula. Far to the east, this action roused the concern of Empress Irene of the Byzantine Empire, which controlled several of Italy's other cities. The Byzantine Empire had grown out of the remains of the eastern portion of the ancient Roman Empire. It included much of Greece and portions of Asia Minor and was centered on the capital in Constantinople. Irene faced a strong alliance between the Franks and the pope in Rome. She could do nothing but watch nervously as Charlemagne extended his reach into Italy and threatened the cities under her control.

Tassilo Surrenders Bavaria to Charlemagne

Charlemagne also had his eye on Bavaria. During his brief marriage to the Lombard princess, Charlemagne had been the brother-in-law of the Bavarian leader, Duke Tassilo. Bavaria linked the Lombard kingdom of northern Italy with the rest of Francia. It was also important because it stood between the eastern Frankish kingdom and a group of people called the Slavs in the Balkans (the mountainous area of southeast Europe that now includes Bosnia, Macedonia, Albania, Bulgaria, and Romania).

In 787, Pope Hadrian I helped Charlemagne take Bavaria. Although the Franks and the Bavarians were not at war, Pope Hadrian told Tassilo's messengers that he wanted Charlemagne and Tassilo to "make peace at once."[12] The pope used his power as a religious leader to frighten Tassilo. He threatened to excommunicate him—to expel him from the Catholic Church and perhaps even damn him to hell. In 787, Charlemagne sent three armies into Bavaria. From the north came an army of Franks and Saxons. From the south came an army from Italy, led by Charlemagne's young son Pepin. From the west came Charlemagne himself. Surrounded on three sides and facing a hopeless battle, Duke Tassilo surrendered. He spent the rest of his life in the monastery at Jumièges, northwest of Paris.

All of the troublesome border kingdoms were now a part of the Frankish Empire. With Francia secure,

Charlemagne looked to the east and prepared for a new enemy: the Avars.

Who Were the Avars?

The Avars were a group of pagan tribes originally from Asia. Their exact origins are a mystery, but at the end of the sixth century they lived in an area between the Danube and Tisa rivers in what is now Hungary. Their capital, called "The Ring," was a circular fortress made of earth and packed with the treasure of their conquered enemies. In 626, the Avars tried to invade the city of Constantinople, and they had terrorized Eastern Europe ever since.

The Avars made the first move in 788, attacking a Frankish army in northern Italy and hitting the borders of Bavaria. Charlemagne responded in 791 with a massive war against them.

The war was well planned: Charlemagne led an army along the south bank of the Danube. An army of Franks and Saxons marched along the north bank of the river. Meanwhile, a fleet of troop and supply ships sailed between the two armies. Charlemagne's son Pepin of Herstal also led an army north through Italy.[13]

When they entered Avar territory, the Franks prepared by spending three days in prayer. After years of battle against the Saxons and faced with the terrifying reputation of Avar warriors, Charlemagne was being as careful as possible.

Source Document

We have ordered solemn prayers from Monday, the fifth of September, to Wednesday, the seventh, imploring God's mercy that He may give us peace, health, victory and a favorable march, and that in His mercy and goodness He will be our helper, guide and defender in all our trials. Our priests have ordered that all who are not hindered by sickness or too great age or youth shall refrain from wine and meat during these days. . . .

Every priest, unless prevented by illness, has been required to say a special Mass, and the clerics who know their psalms have chanted fifty psalms. During these days all the clergy have walked barefoot. Such were the decisions of our clergy, and we are all joined with them and did as they bade with the help of the Lord. . . .

We have been much surprised that we have received no letter from you since we left Regensburg. Write more often about your health and anything else you wish to tell.[14]

Charlemagne's letter to his wife Fastrada in 791 shows the religious preparations the Frankish Army made before doing battle with the Avars.

Surprisingly, the massive Frankish preparations turned out to be unnecessary. When the Avars saw Charlemagne's forces, they abandoned their fortresses and fled. The Franks, expecting a long and bloody war, easily marched into the Avars' western lands.

Complete victory over the Avars seemed close. But the Franks suffered a setback when a strange disease killed most of their horses. The army was forced to return to Francia. Charlemagne had to put off his war with the Avars. In the meantime, he had to deal with many other problems: family matters, religious issues, and old enemies.

Church and State and the Council of Frankfurt

Einhard writes that Charlemagne always had dinner with his sons and daughters whenever he was at home, and that they often went with him on his travels.[1] Just as Charlemagne and his brother Carloman saw much of the Frankish kingdom when they were children, so too did Charlemagne's sons and daughters. Einhard also mentions that Charlemagne never let his daughters get married because he loved them too much. He always wanted them nearby. As a result, there were "a number of unfortunate experiences"[2]—namely, his daughters Rotrud and Bertha had several illegitimate children.[3] Einhard offers a rare glimpse into Charlemagne's home life. When rumors about his daughters surfaced, the king did not listen to the rumors. He pretended not to have heard them or ignored them as gossip.[4]

In 792, another of Charlemagne's children caused him more serious trouble. While the king was away fighting the Avars, his eldest son, Pepin the Hunchback, hatched a conspiracy at home. Pepin had had ten years to stew over the fact that he had been replaced by one of his half-brothers. Einhard says that some other Franks put him up to the conspiracy by offering to make him king. But Einhard does not name names. Since the plot against Charlemagne was probably embarrassing to the Carolingian family, very little is recorded about it.

Whatever the case, the conspirators were not successful, and they were quickly punished. Pepin the Hunchback wanted to sit on the Frankish throne, but his fate was much more humble. He was ordered to become a monk, and he lived out the rest of his days in a monastery.[5] Like Tassilo of Bavaria, Pepin had been outwitted. He had made the mistake of not understanding the Franks' fierce loyalty to Charlemagne himself.

A Saxon Uprising

The following year, Charlemagne decided to finish the war against the Avars. Instead he faced another embarrassment. In 793, after several mostly peaceful years, his old enemies, the Saxons, were rebelling. Charlemagne was spending the autumn of 793 personally overseeing the digging of a canal through the swampy lands between the Danube and the Rhine. If this ambitious project had been completed, Charlemagne would have been able to move ships across a large portion of Europe. A fleet could have traveled from Francia into Bavaria and then into the Avar lands with great ease. But heavy rains ruined Charlemagne's plans when the 300-foot-wide ditch kept filling with mud.[6] The king's disappointment was made worse by the grim news that Frankish troops had been ambushed in Saxony.[7]

The news did not improve. Because Charlemagne was busy with other matters on the eastern end of his kingdom, the Muslim leader of the Spanish city of Cordoba, Hisham I, ordered his forces to take back Gerona—the city on the southern side of the Pyrenees that the Franks had captured only eight years earlier. The Muslim war leader, 'Abd al-Malik ibn Mughith, could not capture Gerona. However, he did cross the Pyrenees to attack the Frankish cities of Narbonne and Carcassonne. Several Frankish nobles were killed, and many more were taken back to Cordoba as captives.[8] Once again, forces from Spain had inflicted an unexpected and humiliating defeat on the Frankish Empire. However, during this time Charlemagne found new ways to defend his Christian religion. In the summer of 794, he held an important meeting: the Council of Frankfurt.

The Council of Frankfurt

Unlike many of Charlemagne's regular Frankish assemblies, the Council of Frankfurt included more religious figures. Bishops and priests came from Spain and Britain, and representatives of the pope made the journey from Rome.

The bishops and priests at the council met in the great hall of the palace at Frankfurt, while Charlemagne's nobles and warlords met elsewhere in the royal villa.[9] In a bold move, Charlemagne himself presided over the assembly—even though he did not have the approval of the pope to oversee the bishops and other religious leaders who were there.

Charlemagne had many matters that he needed to deal with at the council. Some of them were day-to-day concerns in eighth-century Francia. The council made it illegal for anyone to sell crops at extremely high prices; they outlawed bribery among monks; and they made it illegal for priests, monks, and other religious figures to enter taverns to drink.[10] At the council, Charlemagne also introduced new coins. His new silver *denarius* (penny) was made of more silver than other coins at the time and could be used in the whole Frankish kingdom.[11] These coins, which fascinate numismatists (coin collectors) even today, also sent a message to all of Europe that Charlemagne's reign was prosperous.[12] The back of each coin names the location of the mint. The front bears an impressive monogram—a symbol made up of the letters of Charlemagne's name.[13]

Charlemagne also used the Council of Frankfurt to deal with two important religious problems: Adoptionism and iconoclasm.

What Was Adoptionism?

Around 780, a bishop named Elipandus in the Spanish city of Toledo spoke out against a group of heretics—people who were Christians but who held beliefs that did not agree with the teachings of the Catholic Church in Rome.

However, Elipandus was in a province ruled by the Muslim Umayyad dynasty. The authority of the pope, far away in Rome, was very distant indeed. Although he spoke out against the heretics, Elipandus himself said heretical things too. The Catholic Church in Rome believed that Jesus Christ had two natures: he was a man, but he was also divine—the Son of God. Elipandus, on the other hand, believed that Jesus could not be called the Son of God until he was "adopted" by God during his baptism by John the Baptist.[14] In a deeply religious age, detailed and often confusing debates over the nature of Christ—a subject known as Christology—caused strong feelings among Christians. Although Elipandus had meant only to speak out against heresy, he was seen by the rest of the Church in Europe as a heretic himself.

The beliefs of Elipandus, called Adoptionism, became an issue for Charlemagne in 792. Just inside Charlemagne's borders, in the town of Urgell in the eastern Pyrenees, a bishop named Felix said that he supported Elipandus.[15] Because Charlemagne was devoted to the pope and to the beliefs of the Catholic

As royalty, Charlemagne often received gifts from other kingdoms.

Church in Rome, he was very disturbed by the rise of Adoptionism in his own kingdom.

The first order of business at the Council of Frankfurt was to denounce the heretics in the presence of all the bishops and priests. Adoptionism was called "the impious [unholy] and wicked heresy." The council decided that "it should be utterly eradicated from the Holy Church."[16]

What Was Iconoclasm?

During the sixth and seventh centuries, the Byzantine churches far to the east of the Carolingian Empire were using icons: images of Christ, the Virgin Mary, and the saints. Byzantine Christians did not worship these images as if they were God, saints, or angels themselves. Instead they venerated them, meaning that they treated them with respect. They used them to focus on the faith and love of the holy figure in the image. At a time when few people could read or write, icons were a good way to teach people about Christianity with very vivid pictures.

In western Europe, some people thought that the icons were prohibited by God because of the Ten Commandments granted to Moses in the Old Testament of the Bible. The Second Commandment says, "Thou shalt not create graven images," which prohibits people from making statues of other gods or worshiping other gods.

Some people in the Byzantine capital of Constantinople, including Emperor Leo III, agreed that icons were against the Second Commandment. Around 720, he said that he supported iconoclasm, or the destruction of icons. (People who felt that icons should be destroyed were called iconoclasts.) Leo III forbade his subjects from using icons. He may have been influenced by Jewish tradition, which strongly prohibits worshiping images, or Muslim beliefs, which prohibit showing the human form in art.[17] When

Leo III made his announcement, people who venerated icons were attacked, and riots broke out in the streets of Constantinople.[18]

After the death of Leo III, the Byzantine empress, Irene, tried to bring back the use of icons in the 780s. In 787, the Byzantine Church—today known as the Orthodox Church—held the Second Council of Nicea. Four and a half centuries earlier, in 325, early Christians held an important council in this city (in what is now modern Turkey). The Byzantine bishops at the Second Council of Nicea made using icons legal again.

By this time, there was a great deal of competition and conflict between the eastern and western branches of Christianity. The Byzantines believed that their empire was a continuation of the ancient Roman Empire. The religious decisions of Christians in Byzantium did not include the pope in Rome. They held their own church councils without inviting western bishops. Charlemagne saw himself as the equal of the Byzantine emperor. He believed that the western Christian Church, based in Rome, was the true church, so he made decisions about religious issues as well.

Unfortunately, Charlemagne and his bishops did not really understand the decision that had been made at Nicea. The language of the Byzantines was Greek, and only a small handful of the bishops at Frankfurt knew any Greek at all. Because of a very bad translation, Charlemagne and his bishops wrongly believed that the Byzantines wanted people to worship icons as if they were God or Jesus. The Byzantine bishops would not have believed such a thing; it was clearly a heresy. At the council, Charlemagne spoke out against using icons. He then sent a messenger to Pope Hadrian I in Rome to tell him what the council had decided. Hadrian was shocked to learn that Charlemagne had made a religious judgment on his own.[19]

Charlemagne did not think that his role as king meant that he should be only a military leader and king. He also felt very strongly about defending his religion from threats. However, by taking this decision about icons into his own hands without knowing the facts, he only added to the growing divide between churches in western Europe and the Byzantine Empire.

Chapter 7

Building a Frankish Capital

In 795, Charlemagne spent Christmas at his favorite villa in Aachen for the first time in six years. Life at Aachen was busy indeed. Regular raids into Saxony continued, and both good and bad news arrived at the court during this time.

The End of the Avars

Eric, Charlemagne's loyal duke of the Italian city of Friuli, had invaded the land of the Avars. When Eric's troops arrived at "The Ring," the Avars' main fortress, they found that the Avars had been fighting among themselves. Their leader, the *khagan,* had been assassinated. People believed for centuries that "The Ring" could not be captured. However, Eric took advantage of the warfare among the Avars and captured the fortress. He returned to Aachen with vast amounts of treasure that the Avars had won during countless conquests of their own.[1] The following year, at Easter, an Avar leader bearing the mysterious title *tudun* came to Aachen. He surrendered to Charlemagne and led his people to be baptized as Christians.[2] The records of the Carolingians have little to say about the Avars, and their civilization soon disappears from history entirely. About their culture we know almost nothing, except for one detail: the long, flowing hair of the tudun was braided.[3]

New Pope, New Ally

That same year, Charlemagne learned of the death of Pope Hadrian I, his longtime friend and ally. The family of Hadrian I was still very powerful, but the new pope, Leo III, had fewer friends in Rome. Leo knew he needed the protection of the Frankish king, so he immediately wrote to Charlemagne. Charlemagne first helped the new pope in a very practical way: He sent him a large portion of the Avar treasure.

"A Rome Yet to Be"

Although Rome always played an important role in Charlemagne's policies, the king's mind was on Aachen during the 790s. He soon did something that no other Frankish ruler had ever done: He decided to build a permanent capital for his empire—and a permanent home for himself.

Typical of Frankish royalty, Charlemagne grew up traveling from villa to villa. But now that he was nearly fifty-five years old, he was tired, and he loved Aachen. The town had natural hot springs, which were a true luxury in cold medieval Francia.

One poet describes the enthusiastic role that Charlemagne played in the building of the royal palace:

> A second Rome is springing up like a great new flower; it rises high, a powerful structure stretching toward the stars with towering domes and walls. Pious Charles stands there high on its ramparts pointing out particular places and indicating the lofty walls of a Rome yet to be.[4]

The royal palace at Aachen began like a royal villa anywhere in Francia, with a lord's home surrounded by smaller buildings. Stone was brought from all over to build the king's new home, and enough of a palace existed that Charlemagne and his family were able to move in by 795.

Probably inspired by his memories of the Lateran, the pope's palace in Rome, Charlemagne decorated Aachen using the treasures he had gained from his many conquests. A reception hall showed paintings of Charlemagne doing battle in Spain. A statue of Theodoric the Ostrogoth—a barbarian who had conquered Rome—stood in a courtyard. Charlemagne had brought it back from Italy himself.[5] Giant bronze doors with lion's-head handles led to a stunning new church with a sixteen-sided tower and an eight-sided dome that loomed 110 feet overhead. From a throne in the gallery, Charlemagne could look either across to the altar during mass, or up at the dome, where an impressive painting showed Christ sitting in judgment at the end of the world—a reminder of the Christian belief that God was the ultimate ruler of the universe.

Charlemagne connected his palace to the baths by way of a long colonnade—a hallway of pillars covered by a roof. His sturdy stone palace was surrounded by many small wooden buildings, including workshops, homes, a bakery, stables, and granaries. Outside the wall surrounding the palace were the homes of merchants and a market. Nearby, Charlemagne built a walled area where he could relax while hunting wild animals or chasing smaller prey with his falcon.[6]

The Carolingian Renaissance

At Aachen, Charlemagne encouraged learning and education so much that some historians call this time the Carolingian Renaissance, a rebirth of learning and the arts. Einhard says that the king was interested in mathematics, astronomy, and rhetoric—the art of using language to persuade others. He learned Latin and even some Greek.[7]

The great wealth that Charlemagne amassed through conquest allowed him to attract some of Europe's brightest scholars to his court. Chief among them was Alcuin, a monk from the kingdom of Northumbria in northern England. Alcuin was a teacher at the great church in York and was well known not only for his intelligence, but also for the large library he had put together. In 781, Charlemagne and Alcuin crossed paths in the Italian city of Parma when both of them were returning home from journeys to Rome. The king asked the famous scholar to join his court. Except for two return trips to England, Alcuin lived at Charlemagne's court from 782 to 796.

Charlemagne's court also included Peter of Pisa, who specialized in grammar, an Irish scholar named Dungal who was an expert in astronomy, and Paul the Deacon, a historian. At Aachen, Alcuin and his pupils from England mingled with educated men from Francia, Bavaria, and even Spain. Many of these scholars had clever nicknames that showed their respect for learned men of the past. A Frank named Angilbert, for example, was called Homer after the Greek poet known for his ancient epic poems.[8] Charlemagne himself was called David as a reminder of the great Old Testament king often believed to have written the biblical Psalms.[9] For visitors who were thirsty for knowledge and intellectual company, Aachen was a place where they could truly enjoy themselves.

Although some modern historians talk about a "palace school" at Aachen, the term is a bit of an exaggeration.[10] The court at Aachen was always changing. Scholars left to become bishops and abbots somewhere else, while young monks arrived to join the hectic world of Charlemagne's capital. Any visitor looking for a typical classroom would have been very disappointed. Education at Aachen was not formal. Charlemagne's great love of learning, and his busy schedule, meant that a meeting of his learned friends could happen just about anywhere, including the bath house and the royal bedchamber.[11] The king enjoyed poetry and intellectual discussions over a hearty meal with his scholarly friends.[12]

One important result of Charlemagne's emphasis on learning was book production. During the Middle Ages, books were slowly and carefully copied by hand on vellum—animal skin that has been scraped clean and specially prepared. Alcuin writes about *turba scriptorum,* "the crowd of scribes," copying books at Charlemagne's court.[13] Carolingian scholars created beautiful new books, including copies of the Bible, the writings of early Christians, and collections of the Psalms. Alcuin specialized in textbooks on spelling and rhetoric as well as long books on religious issues.[14] Some created books on astronomy, Frankish law, and church law. Others wrote histories or copied books by ancient Roman authors. Some books also included carefully painted illustrations that became examples that other scribes used in creating their own books.

Carolingian monks also created a new handwriting. They replaced the hard-to-read script of the Merovingians with an easier version now called Carolingian minuscule. Over time, this new handwriting became the standard throughout Europe.[15] More than six hundred years later in the fifteenth century, this handwriting was admired by the creators of early printed books during the Italian Renaissance. Carolingian minuscule became the basis for early

"Roman" typefaces—including the kind still used for lowercase letters in most printed books today.[16]

Charlemagne's strong Christian beliefs were a major force behind the Carolingian Renaissance. In a letter known as *De litteris collendis* ("on the study of literature") that was sent throughout Francia at the end of the eighth century, Charlemagne wrote:

> that the bishoprics and monasteries which through the favour of Christ have been entrusted to us to govern should, in addition to the way of life prescribed by their rule and their practice of holy religion, devote their efforts to the study of literature and to the teaching of it.[17]

Charlemagne wanted to make sure that bishops, priests, and monks could read and write so that they could do their jobs well. Just as Charlemagne felt that it was his duty to Christianize the Saxons, he also believed that it was his special role to support learning and intellectual activities that helped his Christian religion.

"A Great Love for Foreigners"

Between 797 and 799, Aachen became a truly international court—and many of the world's controversies arrived on Charlemagne's doorstep. In the autumn of 797, Charlemagne was visited by Abdullah, a Muslim noble from Cordoba who had rebelled against his brother. Around the same time, a messenger arrived with a letter from Constantine VI, the emperor of Byzantium. Constantine VI had been cruelly blinded by orders of his mother, Empress Irene, because he had divorced his wife and married one of his mother's servants.[18] Irene also sent envoys to seek peace with Charlemagne.

Meanwhile, messengers arrived from King Alfonso of the small Spanish kingdoms of Galicia and Asturias. They thanked Charlemagne for some forces he had sent to help them, and they brought gifts that included armor, mules, and prisoners.[19] In 799, two

Constantine VI (right with crown), the emperor of the Byzantine Empire, was blinded by the order of his mother, Irene, because she did not approve of his new marriage.

Mediterranean islands, Mallorca and Menorca, asked for Frankish help. King Hassan of Huesca in northeastern Spain also asked Charlemagne to be his king. In addition, a monk arrived from Jerusalem, bringing greetings from the city's patriarch—the eastern equivalent of a bishop.

In 802, Charlemagne and everyone at Aachen received an extraordinary surprise. Around 797, the king had sent a Jewish envoy named Isaac to Baghdad (in present-day Iraq) to see about forming an alliance with the Muslim caliph—or leader—Harun al-Rashid. Although the two empires were too far away to be of much help to each other, the caliph's response was very generous: Isaac sailed from North Africa to Italy, and then traveled by land to Aachen, with a caravan that included herbs, spices, oils, monkeys, and, most amazing of all, an elephant named Abul Abaz.[20]

At the court, "life was a hurricane," said Paul the Deacon, who left Aachen to return home to Italy as soon as he could.[21] Performers, musicians, and storytellers entertained Charlemagne's many foreign guests, as well as his large family. By 800, Charlemagne had been married at least four times. (During the Middle Ages, it was not uncommon for women to die young, especially because childbirth could be so dangerous.) The king had at least eighteen children by four wives and many mistresses, and at least nine grandchildren.

Byzantine monks, scholars from Ireland, Saxon warriors, messengers from Baghdad, mule trains arriving from the Pyrenees—all contributed to Aachen's mad flurry of activity. Einhard says that Charlemagne "had a great love for foreigners and went to such great pains to entertain them that in all justice their numbers seemed to be a burden not only to the palace but to the whole kingdom."[22]

But Charlemagne was proud to be a Frank and showed his pride through his clothing. According to Einhard, Charlemagne never wore foreign clothing. He hated the loose-fitting outfits of medieval Italy and the puffy pants worn by the nobles in Aquitaine, which was located in present-day southwest France.[23] He wore golden garments and his crown only when he had to appear in public on holy days. Most of the time, the king wore the traditional Frankish outfit: a blue cloak over a tunic, leggings, and cloth leg wrappings. True to his warrior heritage, he always had a sword at his side. Einhard noted that on most days, Charlemagne's clothing looked like that of the common people.[24] Nonetheless, this ruler who loved his Frankish homeland was soon to rise to a position even higher than king: emperor of Rome.

Chapter 8

A King Becomes an Emperor

In the 790s, Aachen flourished as an international capital, but conflict still waited at the northeastern borders of the Frankish Empire. The Saxons rebelled again, so Charlemagne acted decisively—and cruelly.

The Final Wars Against the Saxons

In 794, Charlemagne led his forces into Saxony. The following year he enlisted the aid of the Abrodites, a Slavic people who lived to the east of the Saxons. War between the Franks and the Saxons continued through 799.

In 799, Charlemagne ravaged the entire area between the Weser and the Elbe rivers. He forced the Saxons who lived there to give up their lands. They were scattered throughout the Frankish Empire as slaves, and Charlemagne gave their farmlands to his own loyal nobles. In 804, Charlemagne rounded up all of the Saxons east of the Elbe River and moved them to Francia. Their lands became the property of the Abrodites. The Saxons never again troubled the Franks—but only because Charlemagne's solution was to remove his enemies from their lands.

News From Rome

While he was campaigning against the Saxons in 799, Charlemagne received some alarming news from Rome. His new ally, Pope Leo III, had been attacked while leading a procession between the city's many churches.[1] Family members of the previous pope, Hadrian, resented Leo. For reasons that are not clear, they charged him with two crimes: having sexual relations despite taking vows that he would not, and lying under oath.[2] As punishment, they tried to blind him and cut out his tongue.[3]

Leo was whisked away to a monastery, and although one account says that he was "half-dead and drenched in blood in front of the altar,"[4] he managed to survive with his sight and speech intact. Knowing where to find allies, the pope journeyed to Francia to seek support from Charlemagne.

Charlemagne and the Pope Meet at Paderborn

Charlemagne and Pope Leo III met later that year at Paderborn. The king sent the pope back to Rome with a large number of escorts. Among them were religious

Pope Leo III was attacked by the family of the former pope. He then sought Charlemagne's protection.

---

figures who could investigate the charges against the pope. In August 800, Charlemagne announced that he intended to go to Rome.

Charlemagne Travels to Rome

With his son Charles, Charlemagne and his entourage crossed the Alps and arrived outside Rome by November 800. On Saturday, November 23, 800, Pope Leo III met Charlemagne at the twelfth milestone from the city—the place where the ancient Roman emperors had usually been met before entering Rome.[5]

The next day, Charlemagne entered the city on horseback. During his visits to Rome, Charlemagne was willing to give up his habit of wearing simple Frankish clothing. This time, he wore a long tunic with a Greek mantle—a sleeveless cloak worn over other clothes—and Roman-made shoes. To the people of Rome, Charlemagne needed to be seen as royal and Roman, not as a former barbarian from northern Europe. His daughters were present, probably dressed in their finest clothing.[6]

Crowds lined the streets to behold the Frankish king, and colorful banners decorated the step of the basilica (church) of St. Peter. A basilica, from the Greek for "hall of the king," was a long, rectangular building used by the ancient Romans to house meeting places, courts, and business offices. Early Christians used this style of building for their churches. St. Peter's was built around the year 333 over the place where Peter, the first pope, was believed to be buried.[7] This impressive building was important because it was a reminder not only of Christian history, but also of the ancient traditions and architecture of Rome. It was the perfect place for the many momentous events that occurred that winter.

Charlemagne dismounted at the base of the wide marble stairs. He climbed the stairs, crossed through an open courtyard, and entered the church, all to the sound of chanted Psalms—poems from the Bible.[8] The choir sang, and Charlemagne received communion from the pope during a mass. This was the first of several ceremonies in which the king and the pope cemented their friendship—and quietly defeated their enemies.

One week later, Charlemagne held a public hearing. He announced that he was personally investigating the charges against the pope. For three weeks, he talked to the different sides in Rome. The details of these secret dealings are unknown, but in the end, the long friendship between the Frankish king and the pope won out. On December 23, 800, Pope Leo III swore from the pulpit that he was innocent of all charges. Having sworn this oath in public, and with the powerful Charlemagne as his ally, Leo was safe from further attacks.

The Imperial Coronation

Meanwhile, it was time for Charlemagne to receive something in exchange for sorting out Leo's problems. Two days later, a solemn mass was held to celebrate Christmas. At the basilica of St. Peter, the pope anointed Charlemagne's son Charles, just as his brothers had been anointed by the previous pope in 781, and just as Charlemagne himself had been anointed as a child.

But then the pope did something that would echo in European history for centuries: He placed a crown on Charlemagne's head and declared him emperor. Charlemagne was no longer simply the powerful king of the Franks. He was also emperor of Rome, holder of a title with historic symbolism.

Charlemagne's friend Einhard writes that the king was surprised by the events of Christmas Day, 800: "He made it clear that he would not have entered the cathedral that day at all, although it was the greatest of all the festivals of the Church, if he had known in advance what the Pope was planning to do."[9] However, it was common for ancient and medieval writers to claim that great leaders were so modest that they tried to turn down the powerful positions offered to them.[10] Charlemagne's imperial coronation may have been in the works for quite some time.

Preparing for the Coronation

Modern historians disagree on exactly how much preparation went into Charlemagne's coronation. Some believe that it was hastily put together by Pope Leo to thank Charlemagne for his help and to ensure his help in the future.[11]

Other historians believe that the coronation was the result of a great deal of planning. On the same November day that Pope Leo swore his oath of innocence, Charlemagne received messengers from the patriarch (bishop) of Jerusalem. They brought with them the symbolic keys to the city of Jerusalem and its many holy places.[12] Normally, the patriarch of Jerusalem owed his allegiance to the Byzantine emperor, but far to the east in Byzantium, Empress Irene had murdered her son Constantine and was trying to be the empire's only ruler. That was a difficult, even impossible, role for a woman in the ninth century. Most people did not accept her and considered the throne empty. In the Byzantine Empire, the people saw their empire as a continuation of the ancient Roman Empire—they even considered themselves *Romaioi,* Greek for "Romans."[13] By supporting Charlemagne, the patriarch of Jerusalem, the most holy city in Christianity, was suggesting that Charlemagne was the true Roman emperor.

The Title of Emperor

What did it mean to be the emperor? Christmas Day, 800, found Charlemagne unchanged in most ways from the leader he had been a day earlier. His empire was no larger than it had been, and his power had not increased.

In the end, Charlemagne had to choose his official title delicately. He refused to be called "emperor of the Romans," perhaps because he did not wish to anger the "Romans" of the Byzantine Empire. Instead he chose a more careful title: "Augustus and emperor governing the Roman Empire."[14] Even before Charlemagne returned home from Rome in 800, some written documents already bore a seal that read *"Renovatio Romani imperii"*: "Rebirth of the Roman empire."[15]

The revival of the idea of an emperor created a powerful symbol for centuries to come. Long after Charlemagne's death, Europeans would grow more comfortable with the idea of a "Roman emperor," even if the emperor lived in northern Italy or Germany. This was primarily because the renowned Charlemagne had established the tradition. More than four hundred years after Charlemagne's death, the largely symbolic empire would be given a lasting name: the Holy Roman Empire.

Charlemagne's Final Years

Following an assembly at Aachen in 802, the emperor issued new laws and oaths that applied to all of his subjects across western Europe. Charlemagne wanted his subjects to see themselves as belonging not to a system of scattered kingdoms, but to an empire united under one leader chosen by God.

Charlemagne sent *missi,* or messengers, to the different regions of the empire. The missi were sent out by twos, usually a nobleman with a church official. They told people in each region that they could continue to use their local laws. They also made a note of unfair laws so that Charlemagne could change them, and they acted as fair judges for people who had legal complaints. Now that the king was emperor, the missi also made sure that all Frankish subjects more than twelve years old swore an oath of loyalty to him.[16] By Charlemagne's decree, his subjects were required to respect members of the church and to act morally according to Christian beliefs. For Charlemagne, promoting good behavior among his subjects was simply one of his responsibilities as a Christian emperor, "in order that everything should be good and well-ordered for the praise of Almighty God."[17]

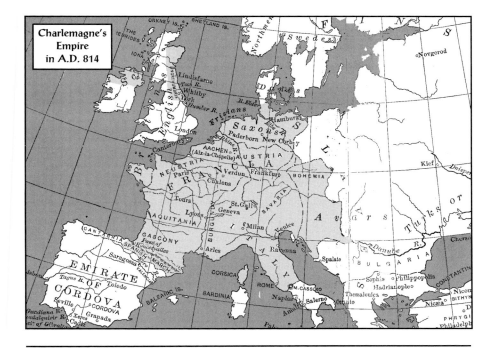

As emperor, Charlemagne ruled over the vast Roman Empire of the West (shaded), which included most of present-day Europe.

Some historians see the last few years of Charlemagne's reign—his years as emperor—as a period of decline.[18] But in fact, the period after Charlemagne's coronation in Rome shows signs of great prosperity because of the unity that his rule brought to western Europe. The Franks constructed mighty fleets of ships. These ships were used to combat Viking raiders from Denmark on the North Sea coast and Arab pirates in the Mediterranean. They were also used to help trade goods. Pottery from the Rhine region was exported to England and other areas of northern Europe, and the work of Frankish glassmakers was in demand in Scandinavia. Meanwhile, the Frankish military was expanding the empire, fighting the Danes in the north and making gains in Bohemia, a land just south of Saxony.

By 806, Charlemagne was more than sixty years old and mindful that his remaining years were short. He also knew, from his experiences with his brother Carloman decades earlier, that when brothers fight over a kingdom, the result is disruption and chaos. That year, he issued a document called the *Divisio regnorum,* in which he clearly said how he wanted his kingdom divided after his death, "So as not to leave my sons a confused and unsettled matter of dispute."[19] His son Louis received eastern and southern France. Pepin of Herstal received the Italian kingdoms, Bavaria, and portions of southern Germany. Charles inherited everything else.

But Charlemagne's careful planning could not take into account the tragedies that would befall his family. In 810, Pepin died at the age of twenty-nine; the following year, Charles died at the age of thirty-nine. Louis, the only royal son of Charlemagne left alive, came to Aachen in 813. Charlemagne, old and frail, appointed Louis coemperor. The event was celebrated with a public announcement and religious services.

With Louis ready to rule the entire Frankish Empire, it seemed as if the dangerous family rivalry that Charlemagne had feared was no longer a concern.

However, the problem had simply been postponed—for Charlemagne's grandchildren.

The Death of Charlemagne

During the winter of 813, Charlemagne became ill with a fever and pains in his side.[20] According to Einhard, a number of signs hinted that the emperor's death was near: eclipses of the sun and moon, earthquakes, and the collapse of a doorway between the palace and the church in Aachen.[21] Einhard also says that during one of his last journeys, Charlemagne was thrown from his horse as a meteor blazed across the sky.[22] "Charlemagne took no notice at all of these portents," says Einhard, "or at least he refused to admit that any of them could have any connexion with his own affairs."[23]

Charlemagne was in his early seventies when he died on January 28, 814. His body was placed in the church at Aachen, where a gold arch and a statue were built over his tomb.[24] An anonymous Carolingian monk mourned his death in poetry:

Woe is me for misery;
Now Charles, voice of majesty and power,
To Aachen's soil she has given,
Woe is me for misery.[25]

After forty-seven years as king of the Franks, including fourteen as emperor of Rome, Charlemagne had conquered most of western Europe. He had defeated enemies such as the Saxons, the Lombards, and the Avars; expanded his empire; and built a capital that had become a home for some of Europe's brightest scholars. He would be remembered for centuries because of these achievements, and his actions would become an important part of European history. It was now time for his empire to pass into other, less capable hands.

Chapter 9

The Holy Roman Empire

Louis was forty-six years old when he inherited the empire from Charlemagne. He was known as Louis the Pious because of his strong religious beliefs. When Louis and his wife Ermengard left their court in Aquitaine to make a permanent home at Aachen, life at the great Frankish palace changed drastically. Louis drove away many of Aachen's entertainers, and he sent his sisters to convents.[1] Like his father, Louis held assemblies to help reform the behavior of religious figures in his empire. He also built many impressive new monasteries.

Louis also shared his father's concern with avoiding civil war, so he imitated his father's solution to the problem. In 817, Louis created a document called the *Ordinatio Imperii,* "Disposition for the Empire." In this document, Louis made his eldest son, Lothair, his

As the new Holy Roman Emperor, Louis the Pious received a coronation ceremony similar to his father's.

coemperor, and he said which parts of the empire his other sons should receive after his death.

The *Ordinatio Imperii* did not solve the problem of rivalry among royal sons. When Louis's wife Ermengard died, he married a woman named Judith who was from a powerful family in the eastern portion of the empire. In 823, Judith gave birth to a son, Charles. Lothair was nervous about the possible rivalry with his half-brother, so he had himself hastily crowned emperor by the pope that same year. Louis also had another son, Louis the German, by a woman named Emma. By 830, the civil war that Louis had tried to avoid had come to pass. Lothair, Charles, and Louis the German—Louis's sons by three different mothers—battled for land and power until their father's death in 840.

The Treaty of Verdun

In 842, Charles and Louis the German joined forces and marched on Aachen, where they took the palace from their half-brother Lothair. For a year, the two

In 823, Lothair had himself crowned emperor, hoping to ensure that he, instead of his newly-born half-brother Charles, would inherit the empire from Louis the Pious.

Louis the German sits on his throne with his sons (right) at his side. Upon Louis's death in 876, his son Carloman would succeed him as King of Bavaria.

victorious brothers negotiated the terms under which they would rule the empire. They then met near Verdun, a town just east of Paris, in 843. The empire was to be divided.

Louis would rule everything east of the Rhine and north of the Alps. Charles would retain everything west of the Scheldt, Meuse, Saône, and Rhône rivers. Louis's kingdom followed the basic borders of modern Germany, and Charles's kingdom traced the borders of what would become modern France.

Their half-brother Lothair was also a part of the plan. Lothair was allowed to keep the title of emperor, and he would rule a central strip of land from the North Sea to the Italian peninsula. These territories eventually became the Netherlands, Belgium, Switzerland, and Italy.

By dividing their empire into these separate regions, Charlemagne's grandchildren were creating the outline for nations that still exist today. One

Charles the Fat (center with crown) only ruled the Holy Roman Empire for six years. After a series of rulers, Otto I became emperor in 962. His family, known as the Ottonians, would rule the empire for over sixty years.

modern historian has called the Treaty of Verdun "the 'birth certificate' of modern Europe."[2] As the western half of the Frankish Empire evolved into France, the imperial title, and the idea of the empire, headed east, to Germany.

The Ottonians Take Control

By the end of the ninth century, the Frankish Empire was in pieces. The power of the Carolingian family ended in 887 when Emperor Charles the Fat, Charlemagne's great-grandson, became ill and stepped down from the throne. In what used to be the Frankish Empire, leaders ruled smaller and smaller kingdoms.

The title of emperor still continued to pass from generation to generation. In the tenth century, it passed to Otto I, who ruled Saxony and parts of northern Italy. Otto and his powerful family—known as the Ottonians—made their capitals the northern Italian cities of Pavia and Ravenna and ruled until 1024. Otto I was the first of many European leaders to idolize Charlemagne. His coronation in 936 was held in an important symbolic location: Aachen. The Ottonians continued to imitate Charlemagne by conquering so-called pagans—the Danes, the Poles, and the Magyars (in what is now modern Hungary)—and converting them to Christianity.

The Ottonians continued Charlemagne's legacy in other ways. Otto III once opened Charlemagne's tomb to take some of his fingernail clippings and one of his teeth, and he even dressed in some of Charlemagne's clothing.[3] The Ottonian emperors supported the arts; built churches, monasteries, and palaces; and hired monks to create many important books. This creative revival, an echo of Charlemagne's hopes for the empire, is sometimes known as the "Ottonian renaissance."[4]

The Investiture Controversy

Since the title of emperor was always changing hands, the relationship between the emperor and the pope was always changing as well—and sometimes led to great clashes. In 1073, a monk named Hildebrand became pope and took the name Gregory VII. The new pope was interested in reforming and strengthening the powers of the Church. A key issue at the time was investiture: the ability to decide who would become a bishop of a town. Kings and emperors believed that they had the right to invest bishops, but popes wanted that right for themselves. Gregory VII and the emperor at the time, Henry IV, king of Germany, both wanted to appoint bishops who would be friendly to their own plans and beliefs. It was Henry IV who made the first bold move in this power struggle.

At a meeting in the German town of Worms in January 1076, Henry IV declared that the pope was not fit to rule. Two bishops who were loyal to Henry IV agreed because they did not want the pope to be able to decide who could hold their positions.[5] In a reply that February, Pope Gregory VII declared Henry IV unfit to rule and excommunicated him.

Wanting to get the upper hand, Henry IV invited the pope to visit him in Germany in 1077. The emperor met the pope halfway, in the Italian city of Canossa. Henry IV did not appear before the pope in his royal garb. Instead he stood barefoot in the winter snow outside the castle gates. He was dressed in the simple rough shirt of a penitent—someone looking for forgiveness from his sins. This simple religious act won the emperor many supporters, and the pope lifted the excommunication.

However, some of the pope's supporters pushed for a new king, and Germany was caught up in a civil war. Henry IV was again excommunicated by the pope. In 1084, Henry IV marched on Rome and replaced Gregory VII with a new pope, Clement III. Gregory VII died in exile in the Italian town of Salerno in 1085, and Henry IV was recognized as the rightful king and emperor.

In 1122, during the reign of Henry IV's son, Henry V, an agreement was reached between royalty and the Church at the town of Worms. This compromise, a peace treaty called the Concordat of Worms, said that since the emperor was also the king of Germany, he was allowed to control the bishops within Germany itself. However, in the other areas of the empire—Burgundy and parts of Italy—he had very little control over church affairs. From the twelfth century onward, the history of the Holy Roman Empire was quickly becoming the history of Germany.

The Hohenstaufen Family and the Holy Roman Empire

In 1152, the title of emperor passed to a German duke from the city of Hohenstaufen named Frederick Barbarossa—a name that meant "red beard." Members of the Hohenstaufen family were related to the Carolingian and Ottonian dynasties, and Frederick saw himself as continuing their work.[6] Some areas of the former empire, such as Italy and Burgundy, had fallen away from the empire. Frederick fought battles to bring them back under the imperial banner. Hoping to revive the empire's former glory, Frederick restored Carolingian and Ottonian palaces. He is also responsible for having Charlemagne canonized, or made into a saint, by the Catholic Church.[7]

During the reign of Frederick Barbarossa, the empire was known as the *Sacrum Imperium,* the Holy Empire. In 1254, under the Hohenstaufen emperor Conrad IV, the empire was given the name it has been remembered by ever since: *Sacrum Romanum Imperium,* or the Holy Roman Empire.[8]

The Hohenstaufen emperors saw themselves as extremely powerful rulers who were at least the equals of the pope. They believed that the judgments, punishments, and decisions made by their empire should be seen as acts of God.[9] Not everyone agreed with this belief. An English writer named John of Salisbury asked: "Who has appointed the Germans judges over the Christian peoples?"[10]

The popes wondered this too. By the early thirteenth century, each new pope was more suspicious of the Hohenstaufen emperors and their growing power. Innocent III, pope from 1198 to 1216, responded with a new idea. He believed that the pope should rule all of the European kings, including the emperor. Kings from many areas, including Portugal, Hungary, Bulgaria, and France, all pledged their loyalty to the pope. Over the course of several decades, these kings wiped out the Hohenstaufen family. In 1268, Conradin, the last Hohenstaufen, was beheaded in Naples.[11] Nearly two hundred years earlier during the Investiture Controversy, the emperor had been more powerful than the pope. Now the papacy had taken firm control of kings and emperors alike.

The Holy Roman Empire had no emperor from 1250 to 1273, but the title of emperor survived—and found a new home with a powerful family called the Hapsburgs.

The Hapsburgs

In 1273, nobles and bishops in the Holy Roman Empire chose Rudolph I to be their new emperor. Rudolph I was a little-known landowner from a family called the Hapsburgs, who were named for a castle in what is now Switzerland.[12] The powerful nobles in the empire probably thought that the unimportant Rudolph I would be their puppet.[13] However, by 1278 Rudolph I had already conquered Bohemia and Austria. Because it held lands at the center of Europe and the title of emperor, the Hapsburg family quickly grew in power. Until the end of the empire in 1806, nearly every emperor was a member of the Hapsburg family.

By the fourteenth century, the Holy Roman Empire covered Germany, Austria, Belgium, the Netherlands, parts of Switzerland, Bohemia, a few lands along the French border, and parts of northern Italy. The Hapsburg emperor Charles IV, who ruled from 1347 to 1378, was impressed by the size of the empire and the number of different European cultures in it. He wrote that "the fame of the Holy Roman Empire arises from the variety of customs, ways of life and language found in the various nations which compose it, and it requires laws and a form of government which pays heed to this variety."[14] But even though he admired the diversity of his European empire, in 1356 he issued a proclamation called the Golden Bull. This proclamation made sure that Germany would continue to be the most powerful nation in the empire.

The Golden Bull set the basic structure of the empire for nearly five hundred years. It dictated that emperors should be elected by seven German dukes, kings, or nobles, and the archbishop of the German city of Metz. Elections were held at Frankfurt, where Charlemagne had held one of his most important assemblies, and the coronation ceremonies took place at Aachen. Because all of the people who appointed the emperor were now important Germans, the pope in Rome had much less power over the empire. By the late 1400s, the empire was even becoming known as the Holy Roman Empire of the German Nation. In 1512, that name became official. The history of the Holy Roman Empire was now, without question, the history of Germany.[15]

Protestantism Divides the Empire

In 1517, a former monk named Martin Luther nailed his Ninety-five Theses, or beliefs, to the door of the cathedral in the German town of Wittenberg. Luther's opinions about Christianity were very controversial. He and his followers became known as Protestants because they protested, or disagreed with, the Catholic Church. They did not believe that the Catholic Church, with the pope as its leader, was the highest authority in Christianity. Instead, they believed that people should use the Bible to make their own choices. They said that faith in God, rather than the rules of bishops, priests, and popes, was the key to Christianity. Protestantism split Christianity—and it split Europe, especially the Holy Roman Empire, as it became more popular.

For a while it seemed as if the empire could hold Catholics and Protestants in peace. In 1555, an agreement called the Religious Peace of Augsburg said Protestants could legally practice their religion in Germany. But tensions between Catholics and Protestants did not end. Their disagreements became part of a larger conflict known as the Thirty Years' War.

Martin Luther started a religious movement in Europe that virtually cut the Holy Roman Empire in two.

The Thirty Years' War

The Thirty Years' War was not a single war, but many revolts, rebellions, and wars that devastated much of Europe. It began in 1618 when the Emperor Matthias—who, like all the emperors, was Catholic—did not allow Protestants to build churches in Bohemia. He also said that Protestants were not allowed to meet and did not have the right to complain to the emperor. On May 23, 1618, angry Protestant nobles came to the emperor's capital in the city of

Prague (now the capital of the Czech Republic) and threw two of Matthias's representatives out of a window.[16] The representatives survived the fall, but the attack set off tensions between Catholics and Protestants that boiled over for thirty years.

In 1619, when Matthias died, Protestant nobles rebelled against the new emperor, Ferdinand I. In 1623, he defeated the rebels, but by 1625 he was faced with the Protestant forces of King Christian IV of Denmark. The Danish were defeated in 1629, but shortly afterward, in 1630, the Swedish king marched into Germany to fight with Protestant princes against the Catholics. In 1635, France joined forces with Sweden and other enemies of the Holy Roman Empire and went to war against the Hapsburgs. Fighting raged across Europe, and the results were disastrous: More than 1 million of Germany's 4 million citizens died, and Bohemia lost nearly half of its 1.7 million people. Many innocent peasants died from diseases spread by traveling armies.[17]

In 1648, the fighting ended with an agreement called the Peace of Westphalia. This agreement gave Protestants rights within the empire—and it also said that each king or prince in the empire could decide what religion his country should officially follow. This was good news for Protestants in Protestant lands, but it also meant that a Catholic emperor could decide that his own lands should be Catholic. By the mid-1600s, most of the nobles in Hapsburg lands had become Catholic.[18]

Some of the worst fighting in European history was now over. It was time for a new flowering of culture in the Holy Roman Empire, especially in its new capital city: Vienna.

Imperial Vienna

The Austrian city of Vienna came under control of the Hapsburgs in 1485. Vienna was an important center of science and trade, but in 1657, under Emperor Leopold I, it also became the imperial city—capital of the Holy Roman Empire.

Leopold I wanted to create a city that was filled with magnificent palaces like those of his rival, King Louis XIV of France. Vienna soon became a major center of a style of architecture called *baroque.* Baroque architecture began in Rome around 1600 and was meant to be so grand and impressive that it overwhelmed the emotions of people who saw it. It was followed by *rococo,* an ornate style with light colors and dainty white and gold decoration. By the mid-1700s, Vienna was a marvelous city of beautiful churches, palaces, monuments, opera houses, and extravagant gardens.

By the 1760s, Vienna also became the music capital of Europe. During the late eighteenth and early nineteenth centuries, important composers such as Wolfgang Amadeus Mozart, Franz Joseph Haydn, Ludwig van Beethoven, and Franz Schubert worked in Vienna. Kings and nobles who had played key roles in religion and politics now hired composers for their courts. Some emperors even composed, played, and conducted music.[19] The symphonies born in Vienna were soon heard in palaces and concert halls as far away as England, helping to create what has been called a golden age of music not only in Vienna, but for all of Europe.[20]

Beyond Vienna, the Holy Roman Empire was still a strong center of culture during the eighteenth century. Germany was home to important writers such as Friedrich von Schiller and Johann Wolfgang von Goethe, and philosophers such as Georg Hegel. The poet and novelist Christoph Wieland, who was born in Germany in 1733, often criticized and mocked the world around him. But even Wieland saw that the empire "provided the framework for the greatest and most unhampered cultural flowering ever to have grown from German soil."[21] Modern historians such as Friedrich Heer agree, calling the late eighteenth century "the great springtime of the intellect" for Germany.[22]

The Decline of the Empire

Even though the Holy Roman Empire was an important center for culture and the arts at the end of the eighteenth century, its power was fading. The empire included Germany, Austria, Bohemia, the Netherlands, Hungary, and even small parts of northern Italy—as well as an always-changing border with France to the west. In 1664, a Dutch politician named Jan de Witt looked at the different nationalities, languages, and religions of the empire and dubbed it "a chimera and a skeleton."[23] (A chimera is a mythical monster made out of the parts of other animals.) The Holy Roman emperor was no longer seen by everyone as the defender of the Catholic Church, because Protestant areas of the empire did not have any ties to the Church. Because some regions were mostly Protestant and others were mostly Catholic, each individual territory or kingdom was becoming more important than the empire as a whole.

The French writer Voltaire, who died in 1778, joked that the Holy Roman Empire was "neither holy, nor Roman, nor an empire."[24] The empire was no longer the only powerful religious force and it seemed to be more of a collection of pieces than an empire. Voltaire's quote predicted the end of the empire—especially since another Frenchman, Napoleon Bonaparte, soon set his sights on Vienna.

Napoleon and the End of the Holy Roman Empire

In France at the end of the eighteenth century, military leader Napoleon Bonaparte rose to power after the French Revolution. Napoleon was obsessed with Charlemagne and his empire.[25] Not content with being leader of the French Republic, Napoleon wanted to conquer all of Europe. In 1804, the French Senate proclaimed him emperor of France. In December 1804, Napoleon put together a ceremony that was based on Charlemagne's coronation more than one thousand years earlier. At the cathedral of

In 1806, Napoleon Bonaparte forced Francis II to give up his crown and end the Holy Roman Empire.

Notre Dame in Paris, with Pope Pius VII nearby, Napoleon was given a crown that supposedly belonged to Charlemagne.[26]

In Vienna, Emperor Francis II was the true heir to the Holy Roman Empire, but he was no match for Napoleon. In 1805, Napoleon's forces defeated the emperor's Austrian Army. Napoleon demanded that the emperor step down. On August 6, 1806, Francis II gave up the crown and ended the Holy Roman Empire. Napoleon reorganized most of Germany as he saw fit. An empire that had survived in some form for more than one thousand years was brought to a swift end.

Chapter 10

The Legacy of Charlemagne and the Holy Roman Empire

Even though the Holy Roman Empire was dissolved in 1806, the idea of the empire survived into the twentieth century. From 1933 to 1945, Adolf Hitler and the Nazis called their regime in Germany the Third Reich (*reich* is German for "nation" or "kingdom"). To the Nazis, the First Reich had been the Holy Roman Empire begun by Charlemagne with his coronation by the pope on Christmas Day, 800. The Second Reich was Germany after the fall of the empire.[1] According to Albert Speer, chief Nazi architect, Hitler once sat at his home within view of a mountain called the Untersberg. A German legend claimed that Charlemagne slept inside the mountain and would one day arise to restore the German Empire. Intent on conquering Europe, Hitler saw himself as the heir to Charlemagne's legend. "You see the Untersberg over there," Hitler once said to Speer. "It is no accident that I have my residence opposite it."[2]

With dreams of conquest, Hitler and the Nazis attempted to conquer Europe during World War II, until they were stopped by the Allied forces—including Britain and the United States—in 1945. Before and during the war, Hitler and the Nazis were responsible for the murder of over 11 million people, mostly civilians. Six million of those killed were Jews. This mass murder has come to be known as the Holocaust.

In 1949, an Aachen merchant, Dr. Kurt Pfeiffer, tried to look beyond the destruction and death that the Nazis and Hitler had caused. Hoping to show the legacy of Charlemagne in a more positive light, Pfeiffer created a prize "for persons who had rendered distinguished service on behalf of West European unification, humanity and world peace."[3] Since then, the Charlemagne Prize has been awarded at Aachen to leaders such as Winston Churchill, prime minister of Great Britain, and Václav Havel, president of the Czech Republic.[4]

During the 1950s, several western European nations—Belgium, France, West Germany, Italy, Luxembourg, and the Netherlands—banded together to form the European Community.[5] The history of the

Charlemagne's vision of a united Europe is at least partially being realized in the formation of the European Union.

Carolingian Empire and the influence of the Treaty of Verdun were very clear: The map of those six founding countries of the European Community covered the same area as Charlemagne's empire.[6] The European Community is now the European Union, which works for economic and social progress, a single currency, and laws that cover all of the member countries.[7] The capital of the European Union is the Belgian city of Brussels[8]—located only 70 miles from Aachen. A hint of the medieval roots of the European Union is found in the name of one of their most important centers in Brussels: the Charlemagne Building.

Writing shortly after Charlemagne's death in the ninth century, a Carolingian monk named Walafrid Strabo summed up the great deeds of the legendary king and emperor: "Thereby with God's help he made his kingdom, which was dark and almost wholly blind . . . radiant with the blaze of fresh learning, hitherto [earlier] unknown to our barbarians."[9]

More than one thousand years later, many historians agree with Strabo's praise of Charlemagne's role in history. According to Allen Cabaniss,

> [i]n some sense therefore it is true to state that European (that is, Western) civilization was launched by Charlemagne on its triumphal way down the centuries, the impact of which is not yet entirely lost; and he himself has entered the full stream of European song, folklore, liturgy [church ritual] and political tradition as one of its dominant personalities.[10]

Historian Friedrich Heer agrees that the empire of Charlemagne set the stage for more than one thousand years of European history:

> Charles the Great [Charlemagne] built up a European empire which fell apart soon after his death. Yet structures from Carolingian Europe determined the basic features of European political and social life and the institutions of the church, culture and education in Europe until 1806, and were still an influence down to 1914.[11]

On the other hand, historian Heinrich Fichtenau points out that for centuries, when people have looked back at Charlemagne's empire and the Holy Roman Empire that followed it, they have seen only what they wanted to see:

> Thus the empire of the Franks and its mighty emperor became the symbols of splendour and greatness. The darker aspects were consigned [sent] to oblivion. It is human to overlook what is all too human.[12]

Charlemagne inspired power-hungry military leaders as well as peaceful prime ministers. His legacy is the dream of European unity. Twelve centuries later, this dream remains very much alive.

Timeline

c. 600 –717—The Frankish kingdoms are ruled by a dynasty known as the Merovingians; Charlemagne's ancestors hold powerful positions in the palaces of the Frankish kings.

717 –719—Charlemagne's grandfather, Charles Martel, controls the Merovingian kings; He becomes the ruler of Francia, although the kings themselves remain on the throne.

741—Charles Martel dies; His sons Pepin III and Carloman run the kingdom, even though a Merovingian king continues to sit on the throne.

747—Carloman retires to a monastery.

750—Pepin III sends the Merovingian king to a monastery and becomes the true king of the Franks.

754—Pepin III's son Charlemagne first appears in recorded history around the age of twelve, escorting Pope Stephen II to a Frankish villa.

768—Pepin III dies, leaving the kingdom divided between his sons, Charlemagne and Carloman.

771—Carloman dies; Charlemagne takes control of his lands.

772—Charlemagne mounts his first campaign against the Saxons and destroys a famous religious shrine, the Irminsul.

773—Saxons attack the church of St. Boniface; Charlemagne responds with a major invasion of Saxony.

774—After a ten-month siege, the Franks defeat the Lombards.

775—Saxons ambush a Frankish camp, prompting more bitter warfare.

778—Charlemagne marches into Spain, but the Muslim leaders who requested his aid are no longer in power; During his retreat, Basques ambush the Frankish army in the Pyrenees mountains.

779 –780—Charlemagne forcibly baptizes many Saxons on the banks of the River Oker.

781—Charlemagne visits Rome.

782—When Frankish forces are defeated in the Süntel Mountains, Charlemagne marches into Saxony and beheads four thousand five hundred Saxons.

785—The Saxons surrender; Widukind, a Saxon leader, is baptized.

791—Charlemagne plans a full war against the Avars; Massive Frankish forces march into Avar territory.

794—Charlemagne organizes the Council of Frankfurt.

795—Charlemagne and his family move in to the new palace at Aachen; Eric, an Italian duke loyal to Charlemagne, conquers the Avars and brings their treasure to Aachen.

797 –799—Aachen becomes a truly international court, with scholars from Ireland, Britain, and Italy, and visitors from Spain, Byzantium, and Jerusalem.

800—Charlemagne travels to Rome to investigate an attack against the pope. On Christmas Day, Charlemagne is crowned emperor.

804—Charlemagne finishes his takeover of Saxony.

806—Charlemagne divides the empire between his three royal sons: Louis, Charles, and Pepin of Herstal.

810—Charlemagne's son Pepin of Herstal dies.

811—Charlemagne's son Charles dies.

813—Charlemagne's son Louis the Pious comes to Aachen, where he becomes coemperor with his father.

814—Charlemagne dies and is buried at Aachen; Louis the Pious inherits the empire.

830 –840—The three sons of Louis the Pious battle for land and power until Louis's death.

842—The Treaty of Verdun divides Europe between the three sons of Louis the Pious.

887—Charles the Fat, Charlemagne's great-grandson, steps down from the throne due to illness, ending Carolingian power in Europe.

919 –1024—The Ottonians, a German dynasty, inherit the imperial title and imitate some aspects of Charlemagne's reign.

1073 –1077—During the Investiture Controversy, Pope Gregory VII and Emperor Henry IV argue over who has the power to appoint bishops.

1152—The Hohenstaufen family inherits the title of emperor, beginning with Frederick Barbarossa; He has Charlemagne named a saint and restores Carolingian and Ottonian palaces.

1254—The term *Sacrum Romanum Imperium,* Holy Roman Empire, is used for the first time under Emperor Conrad IV.

1273—The Hapsburg family begins its rule of the Holy Roman Empire.

1356—Emperor Charles IV issues the Golden Bull, a proclamation that describes how an emperor should be chosen; It is used for nearly five hundred years.

1512—The official name of the empire becomes "The Holy Roman Empire of the German Nation."

1618—In a series of rebellions against the emperor,
–1648 Protestants and Catholics battle across Europe during the Thirty Years' War.

1657—The Austrian city of Vienna becomes the capital of the Holy Roman Empire.

1750—Vienna becomes a major center of art,
–1800 architecture, and especially music.

1804—In Paris, France, Napoleon Bonaparte is crowned emperor of France in a ceremony that imitates Charlemagne's Roman coronation more than one thousand years earlier.

1806—Napoleon defeats the Austrian Army and forces Emperor Francis II to give up his crown; The Holy Roman Empire is dissolved.

1933—Adolf Hitler and the German Nazi party
–1945 call their regime the Third Reich, based on their belief that the Holy Roman Empire established by Charlemagne was the First Reich.

1949—After World War II, a merchant from Aachen creates the Charlemagne Prize, an award for European leaders who promote unity and world peace.

1950s—Several western European nations band together to form the European Community, which covers roughly the same area that Charlemagne's empire did eleven hundred years earlier.

1993—With several new member nations, the European Community is renamed the European Union; It is headquartered in the Charlemagne Building in Brussels, Belgium—only seventy miles from Aachen.

Chapter Notes

Chapter 1. A New Roman Emperor

1. Bernhard Walter Scholz, trans., *Carolingian Chronicles: Royal Frankish Annals and Nithard's Histories* (Ann Arbor Paperbacks: University of Michigan Press, 1970), p. 81.

2. "Franks," *Encyclopedia Britannica* online, <http://www.britannica.com/eb/article?idxref=464395> (March 30, 2001).

3. Roger Collins, *Charlemagne* (University of Toronto Press, 1998), p. 35; Pierre Riché, *The Carolingians: A Family Who Forged Europe* (Philadephia: University of Pennsylvania Press, 1993), p. 5.

4. R. W. Southern, *The Making of the Middle Ages* (New Haven, Conn.: Yale University Press, 1953), p. 135.

5. Josiah Cox Russell, *Late Ancient and Medieval Population* (Philadelphia: Transactions of the American Philosophical Society, Vol. 48, Part 3, 1958), pp. 73, 93.

6. Southern, p. 135.

7. Ibid.

8. Ibid.

9. Frederick Brittain, trans., *Penguin Book of Latin Verse* (London: Penguin Books, 1962), p. 155, in Chris Nyborg, "The Churches of Rome," <http://home.online.no/~cnyborg/poem.html> (March 30, 2001).

10. Chris Wickham, *Early Medieval Italy: Central Power and Local Society 400–1000* (Ann Arbor Paperbacks, University of Michigan Press 1981), p. 164.

Chapter 2. Heir to an Empire

1. J. M. Wallace-Hadrill, trans., *The Fourth Book of the Chronicle of Fredegar with its Continuations* (London: Thomas Nelson and Sons Ltd., 1960), p. 104.

2. Wallace-Hadrill, p. 104.

3. Pierre Riché, *Daily Life in the World of Charlemagne* (Philadelphia: University of Pennsylvania Press, 1996), pp. 41–42.

4. Allen Cabaniss, *Charlemagne* (New York: Twayne Publishers, 1972), p. 3.

5. Riché, p. 225.

6. Donald Bullough, *The Age of Charlemagne* (New York: Exeter Books, 1980), p. 11.

7. J. M. Wallace-Hadrill, *The Long-Haired Kings* (University of Toronto Press/Medieval Academy Reprints for Teaching 11, 1982), p. 84.

8. Lewis Thorpe, trans., *Einhard and Notker the Stammerer: Two Lives of Charlemagne* (New York: Penguin Classics, 1969), p. 55.

9. Pierre Riché, *The Carolingians: A Family Who Forged Europe* (Philadelphia: University of Pennsylvania Press, 1993), p. 53; Wallace-Hadrill, *The Long-Haired Kings,* p. 232.

10. Riché, *The Carolingians,* p. 26.

11. Ibid., p. 27.

12. Ibid., pp. 34–35.

13. Ibid., p. 46.

14. Wallace-Hadrill, *The Fourth Book of the Chronicle of Fredegar,* p. 100.

15. Bernhard Walter Scholz, trans., Carolingian *Chronicles: Royal Frankish Annals and Nithard's Histories* (Ann Arbor Paperbacks, The University of Michigan Press, 1970), p. 39.

16. Riché, *The Carolingians,* p. 69.

Chapter 3. Franks and Lombards

1. Bernhard Walter Scholz, trans., *Carolingian Chronicles: Royal Frankish Annals and Nithard's Histories* (Ann Arbor Paperbacks/University of Michigan Press, 1972), p. 182, n. 2.

2. Lewis Thorpe, trans., *Einhard and Notker the Stammerer: Two Lives of Charlemagne* (New York: Penguin Classics, 1969), p. 59.

3. Scholz, p. 48.

4. Ibid., p. 182, n. 1.

5. Pierre Riché, *The Carolingians: A Family Who Forged Europe* (Philadelphia: University of Pennsylvania Press, 1993), p. 101.

6. Roger Collins, *Charlemagne* (University of Toronto Press, 1998), p. 40.

7. Thorpe, p. 58.

8. Mikel V. Ary, "The Politics of the Frankish-Lombard Marriage Alliance," *Archivum Historiae Pontificiae,* 19, 1981, pp. 7–26.

9. Ibid., p. 20.

10. Ibid., p. 24.

11. Thorpe, p. 162.

12. Collins, p. 60.

13. Scholz, pp. 49–50.

14. Riché, *Daily Life in the World of Charlemagne* (Philadelphia: University of Pennsylvania Press, 1996), p. 78.

15. Ibid., p. 80.

16. Collins, p. 61.

17. "Medieval Sourcebook: The Monk of St. Gall: The Life of Charlemagne, 883/4," <http://www.fordham.edu/halsall/basis/stgall-charlemagne.html> (April 5, 2001). From A. J. Grant, ed. and trans., *Early Lives of Charlemagne* by Eginhard and the Monk of St. Gall (London: Chatto and Windus, 1926), pp. 146–147.

18. Collins, p. 61.

Chapter 4. At War With the Saxons

1. Lewis Thorpe, trans., *Einhard and Notker the Stammerer: Two Lives of Charlemagne* (New York: Penguin Classics, 1969), p. 61.

2. J. M. Wallace-Hadrill, trans., *The Fourth Book of the Chronicle of Fredegar with its Continuations* (London: Thomas Nelson and Sons Ltd., 1960), p. 31.

3. Roger Collins, *Charlemagne* (University of Toronto Press, 1998), p. 45.

4. Thorpe, pp. 79–80.

5. Collins, p. 46.

6. Pierre Riché, *The Carolingians: A Family Who Forged Europe* (Philadelphia: University of Pennsylvania Press, 1993), p. 103.

7. Bernhard Walter Scholz, *Carolingian Chronicles: Royal Frankish Annals and Nithard's Histories* (Ann Arbor Paperbacks/University of Michigan Press, 1972), pp. 48–49.

8. Ibid., p. 51.

9. Ibid., p. 50.

10. Ibid., p. 53.

11. Ibid., p. 55.

12. Collins, p. 49.

13. Scholz, p. 55.

Chapter 5. Expanding the Empire

1. Roger Collins, *Charlemagne* (University of Toronto Press, 1998), pp. 65–66.

2. Ibid., pp. 66–67.

3. Bernhard Walter Scholz, *Carolingian Chronicles: Royal Frankish Annals and Nithard's Histories* (Ann Arbor Paperbacks/University of Michigan Press, 1972), p. 56.

4. Ibid., p. 58.

5. Collins, p. 69.

6. Ibid., p. 70.

7. Scholz, p. 60.

8. Ibid., p. 61.

9. Ibid., p. 62.

10. Collins, p. 70.

11. Scholz, p. 63.

12. Ibid., p. 64.

13. Pierre Riché, *The Carolingians: A Family Who Forged Europe* (Philadelphia: University of Pennsylvania Press, 1993), p. 108.

14. Richard Winston, *Charlemagne: From the Hammer to the Cross* (New York: The Bobbs-Merrill Company, Inc., 1954), p. 201.

Chapter 6. Church and State and the Council of Frankfurt

1. Lewis Thorpe, *Einhard and Notker the Stammerer: Two Lives of Charlemagne* (New York: Penguin Books, 1969), p. 75.

2. Ibid.

3. Ibid., p. 185, n. 55.

4. Ibid., p. 75.

5. Ibid.

6. Bernhard Walter Scholz, trans., *Carolingian Chronicles: Royal Frankish Annals and Nithard's Histories* (Ann Arbor Paperbacks/University of Michigan Press, 1972), p. 71.

7. Scholz, p. 72.

8. Allen Cabaniss, *Charlemagne* (New York: Twayne Publishers, Inc., 1972), pp. 65–66.

9. Donald Bullough, *The Age of Charlemagne* (London: Elek Books Limited, 1965), p. 162.

10. H. R. Loyn and John Percival, *The Reign of Charlemagne: Documents on Carolingian Government and Administration* (New York: St. Martin's Press, 1975), pp. 57–60.

11. Pierre Riché, *The Carolingians: A Family Who Forged Europe* (Philadelphia: University of Pennsylvania Press, 1993), p. 320.

12. Heinrich Fichtenau, *The Carolingian Empire* (University of Toronto Press/Medieval Academy Reprints for Teaching, 1978), pp. 79–80.

13. Pierre Riché, *Daily Life in the World of Charlemagne* (Philadelphia: University of Pennsylvania Press, 1978), p. 125.

14. Jaroslav Pelikan, *The Growth of Medieval Theology (600–1300)* (University of Chicago Press, 1978), pp. 54–56.

15. Roger Collins, *Charlemagne* (University of Toronto Press, 1998), p. 130.

16. Loyn and Percival, p. 57.

17. George Ostrogorsky, *History of the Byzantine State* (New Brunswick, N.J.: Rutgers University Press, 1969), p. 161.

18. Margaret Deanesly, *A History of the Medieval Church, 590–1500* (New York: Routledge, 1969), p. 74.

19. Riché, *The Carolingians,* p. 349.

Chapter 7. Building a Frankish Capital

1. Roger Collins, *Charlemagne* (University of Toronto Press, 1998), p. 95.

2. Bernhard Walter Scholz, trans., *Carolingian Chronicles: Royal Frankish Annals and Nithard's Histories* (Ann Arbor Paperbacks/University of Michigan Press, 1972), pp. 74–75.

3. Allen Cabaniss, *Charlemagne* (New York: Twayne Publishers, 1972), pp. 78-79.

4. Ibid., pp. 80–81.

5. Richard E. Sullivan, *Aix-la-Chapelle in the Age of Charlemagne* (Norman: University of Oklahoma Press, 1963), pp. 57–58.

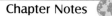

6. Pierre Riché, *Daily Life in the World of Charlemagne* (Philadelphia: University of Pennsylvania Press, 1978), p. 96.

7. Lewis Thorpe, *Einhard and Notker the Stammerer: Two Lives of Charlemagne* (New York: Penguin Books, 1969), p. 79.

8. Donald Bullough, *The Age of Charlemagne* (London: Elek Books Limited, 1965), p. 102.

9. Sullivan, p. 83.

10. Giles Brown, "Introduction: The Carolingian Renaissance," *Carolingian Culture: Emulation and Innovation,* ed. Rosamund McKitterick (New York: Cambridge University Press, 1994), pp. 31–32.

11. Sullivan, p. 83.

12. Heinrich Fichtenau, *The Carolingian Empire* (University of Toronto Press/Medieval Academy Reprints for Teaching, 1978), p. 92; Sullivan, pp. 76–77.

13. Florentine Mütherich and Joachim E. Gaehde, *Carolingian Painting* (New York: The Metropolitan Museum of Art, 1976), p. 8.

14. Bullough, p. 104.

15. Mütherich and Gaehde, p. 8.

16. Bullough, pp. 127–128; McKitterick, p. 233.

17. H. R. Loyn and John Percival, *The Reign of Charlemagne: Documents on Carolingian Government and Administration* (New York: St. Martin's Press, 1975), p. 63.

18. Cabaniss, p. 82.

19. Sullivan, p. 85.

20. Ibid., p. 86.

21. Ibid., p. 152.

22. Ibid., p. 85.

23. Riché, p. 162.

24. Thorpe, p. 78.

Chapter 8. A King Becomes an Emperor

1. Roger Collins, *Charlemagne* (Toronto: University of Toronto Press, 1998), pp. 141–142.

2. Ibid.

3. "Pope St. Leo III," *The Catholic Encyclopedia* online, <http://www.newadvent.org/cathen/09157b.htm> (April 12, 2001).

4. Collins, p. 142.

5. Ibid., p. 145.

6. Heinrich Fichtenau, *The Carolingian Empire* (University of Toronto Press/Medieval Academy Reprints for Teaching, 1978), p. 42.

7. Edward Foley, *From Age to Age: How Christians Have Celebrated the Eucharist* (Chicago: Liturgy Training Publications, 1991), p. 46.

8. Allen Cabaniss, *Charlemagne* (New York: Twayne Publishers, Inc., 1972), p. 93.

9. Lewis Thorpe, *Einhard and Notker the Stammerer: Two Lives of Charlemagene* (New York: Penguin Books, 1969), p. 81.

10. Collins, p. 144.

11. Cabaniss, p. 100.

12. Collins, p. 146.

13. Ibid., p. 150.

14. Pierre Riché, *The Carolingians: A Family Who Forged Europe* (Philadelphia: University of Pennsylvania Press, 1993), p. 122.

15. Donald Bullough, *The Age of Charlemagne* (London: Elek Books Limited, 1965), p. 184.

16. H. R. Loyn and John Percival, *The Reign of Charlemagne: Documents on Carolingian Government and Administration* (New York: St. Martin's Press, 1975), pp. 81–82.

17. Ibid., p. 79.

18. Collins, p. 171.

19. Riché, p. 134.

20. Thorpe, p. 84.

21. Ibid.

22. Ibid., p. 85.

23. Ibid., p. 86.

24. Ibid., p. 84.

25. Eleanor Shipley Duckett, *Carolingian Portraits: A Study in the Ninth Century* (Ann Arbor: University of Michigan Press, 1962), p. 19.

Chapter 9. The Holy Roman Empire

1. Pierre Riché, *The Carolingians: A Family Who Forged Europe* (Philadelphia: University of Pennsylvania Press, 1993), p. 146.

2. Ibid., p. 168.

3. Friedrich Heer, *The Holy Roman Empire* (New York: Frederick A. Praeger, 1968), p. 44.

4. Keith Sidwell, *Reading Medieval Latin* (New York: Cambridge University Press, 1995), pp. 151–152.

5. Uta-Renate Blumenthal, *The Investiture Controversy: Church and Monarchy from the Ninth to the Twelfth Century* (Philadelphia: University of Pennsylvania Press, 1988), p. 121.

6. Heer, p. 68.

7. Ibid.

8. "Holy Roman Empire," *Encyclopedia Britannica* online <http://www.britannica.com/eb/article?eu= 109232&tocid=10156#10156.toc> (April 21, 2001).

9. Heer, p. 76.

10. Ibid., p. 77.

11. Ibid., p. 87.

12. Ibid., p. 96.

13. Charles W. Ingrao, *The Hapsburg Monarchy 1618–1815,* 2nd ed. (New York: Cambridge University Press, 2000), p. 3.

14. Heer, p. 116.

15. Peter H. Wilson, *The Holy Roman Empire 1495–1806* (New York: St. Martin's Press, 1997), p. 9.

16. Ronald G. Asch, *The Thirty Years War: The Holy Roman Empire and Europe, 1618-1648* (New York: St. Martin's Press, 1997), p. 47.

17. Ingrao, p. 49.

18. Ibid., p. 51.

19. Heer, p. 239.

20. "Vienna," *Encyclopedia Britannica,* 15th ed., vol. 29, p. 497.

21. Heer, p. 266.

22. Ibid.

23. Ibid., p. 224.

24. "Holy Roman Empire," *Wikipedia* <http://www.wikipedia.com/wiki/Holy_Roman_Empire> (November 20, 2001).

25. David Nicholls, *Napoleon: A Biographical Companion* (Santa Barbara, Calif.: ABC-CLIO, 1999), p. 179.

26. Owen Connelly, *Blundering to Glory: Napoleon's Military Campaigns* (Wilmington, Del.: Scholarly Resources, Inc., 1987), p. 77.

Chapter 10. The Legacy of Charlemagne and the Holy Roman Empire

1. "Third Reich," *Encyclopedia Britannica* online <http://www.britannica.com/eb/article?eu=74020> (April 21, 2001).

2. Albert Speer, *Inside the Third Reich* (New York: The Macmillan Company, 1970), p. 86.

3. "The Charlemagne Prize: Speech by Prof. Dr. Walter Eversheim at the ceremony marking the 50th

anniversary of the Charlemagne Prize on December 16, 1999, in the Coronation Hall of the Aachen Town Hall," <http://194.245.36.141/karlspreis2000/default_eng. htm> (April 21, 2001).

4. "The Charlemagne Prize 2000": <http://194. 245.36.141/karlspreis2000/default_eng.htm> (April 21, 2001).

5. "European Union," *Encyclopedia Britannica* online <http://www.britannica.com/eb/article?eu= 33850&tocid=0> (April 21, 2001).

6. Gilbert Trausch, "Consciousness of European identity after 1945," in Thomas Jansen, ed., *Reflections on European Identity* (European Commission Forward Studies Unit Working Paper, 1999), p. 25 <http:// europa.eu.int/comm/cdp/working-paper/european_ identity_en.pdf> (January 7, 2002).

7. "The ABCs of the European Union" <http:// europa.eu.int/abc-en.htm> (April 21, 2001).

8. "Brussels: Capital of the European Union" <http://www.trabel.com/brussel/brussels-european union.htm> (April 21, 2001).

9. Richard E. Sullivan, *Aix-la-Chapelle in the Age of Charlemagne* (Norman: University of Oklahoma Press, 1963), p. 148.

10. Allen Cabaniss, *Charlemagne* (New York: Twayne Publishers, Inc., 1972), p. 141.

11. Friedrich Heer, *The Holy Roman Empire* (New York: Frederick A. Praeger, 1968), p. 9.

12. Heinrich Fichtenau, *The Carolingian Empire* (University of Toronto Press/Medieval Academy Reprints for Teaching, 1978), p. 188.

Further Reading

Biel, Timothy L. *The Importance of Charlemagne*. San Diego: Lucent Books, 1997.

Bullfinch, Thomas. *Bullfinch's Mythology: The Age of Fable, the Age of Chivalry, Legends of Charlemagne*. New York: HarperCollins, 1991.

LeBrun, Francoise, and Ginette Hoffmann. *The Days of Charlemagne*. Englewood Cliffs, N.J.: Silver Burdett Press, 1985.

MacDonald, Fiona. *The World in the Time of Charlemagne*. Broomall, Pa.: Chelsea House Publishers, 2000.

Sayers, Dorothy L., trans. *The Song of Roland*. New York: Penguin Classics, 1957.

Thorpe, Lewis, trans. *Einhard and Notker the Stammerer: Two Lives of Charlemagne*. New York: Penguin Classics, 1969.

Internet Addresses

"About the City of Aachen." 2000. <http://www-i5. informatik.rwth-aachen.de/mjf/stadt-aachen. html>

Ingrao, Charles W. "Holy Roman Empire." *DiscoverySchool.com: A-to-Z History.* 2001. <http://school.discovery.com/homeworkhelp/ worldbook/atozhistory/h/260160.html>

Turner, Samuel Epps, trans. "Einhard: The Life of Charlemagne." *The Online Reference Book for Medieval Studies: Medieval Sourcebook.* n.d. <http://www.fordham.edu/halsall/basis/einhard. html>

Index